THE GET TO THE POINT! GUIDE TO MICROSOFT WORD 2016

THE GET TO THE POINT! GUIDE TO MICROSOFT WORD 2016

MARC ALLAN MOORE

CONTENTS

INTRODUCTION

Let's be honest: there are many reasons to use Microsoft Word 2016, but often there's only one that matters: because you have to. Even those who hate Word and profess wanting it to 'die' will concede that their hostility springs from the program's ubiquity—for many today, Word is essentially unavoidable. An estimated half a billion people use some version of Word as part of their normal routine, orders of magnitude ahead of its nearest competitor.

For better or for worse, Word virtually defines the standard for word processing—and perhaps more importantly, creation of standardized documents. So many venues require delivery in Word .doc and .docx formats that to list them here would be prohibitively lengthy, not to mention tiresome. And while it may not surprise you that this book was created and submitted entirely using Microsoft Word 2016, you might be shocked to find that many of your favorite authors likely used Word to draft their most famous works.

But whether you like it, love it, or hate it, chances are that Microsoft Word is here to stay for the foreseeable future—so as long as we have to deal with it, let's make it as easy, comfortable, and painless as possible. Fortunately, while Microsoft Word 2016 is a behemoth of a program boasting a dizzying array of powerful tools, few users will ever need to use more than a fraction of its immense capabilities. Therefore, the overwhelming majority of people can comfortably sustain a typical academic, office, or corporate career after having mastered only a few basic techniques—and mastering those simple techniques is precisely the point of the ***Get to the Point!* Guide to Microsoft Word 2016**.

Within these pages, I've boiled down a lifetime of experience using Microsoft Word as a professional technical writer to just the commands, techniques, and secrets you're likely to use on a daily basis, in order to get you up and running with Word as rapidly as possible without getting bogged down in page after page of impossible-to-remember keystroke combinations or obscure formatting marks that only professional graphic designers and typesetters generally know about.

Instead, you may be surprised to find just how quickly you can learn the relatively small percentage of useful commands most users use on a regular basis, weaving them into a comfortable workflow you can slide easily into each workday—and if those are the only techniques you ever need, you'll be set for life! However, if like most users you do find occasional need for more advanced formatting outside your basic Word mastery, don't worry—we will provide solutions to cover such circumstances as well.

Of course, if your job requires routine use of Microsoft Word 2016's more advanced features such as macros or your installation is heavily customized with a variety of add-ins or other modifications, you might be better served with a more comprehensive book, as this ***Get to the Point!* Guide to Microsoft Word 2016** is intended for the day-to-day user who needs to use the program for typical academic or office purposes. But whether you're a complete novice to the program or a casual user who has never dipped their toe further than a few familiar commands, chances are you'll find something here to simplify your workflow, speed your work, and get on with your day.

CHAPTER 1

A NOTE REGARDING APPLE MACS

AS WORD HAS EVOLVED over the years, the differences between PC and Mac versions of the software have eroded to the point of virtual invisibility—though variances still exist, the Mac version of Microsoft Word 2016 brings the program in line with its comparable Windows version, so in practical terms the programs can be used more or less interchangeably. As you will notice, this book does not heavily emphasize keyboard shortcuts or other platform-specific details, but if you are using a Mac you are probably already quite aware that slight differences often pop up between Windows and OSX software. I myself use both platforms regularly, and the advice in this book has been tested thoroughly to apply equally.

For the most part, as long as you keep the typical Mac substitutions in mind (**Ctrl** on Windows → **Command** on Mac, **Enter** → **Return**, etc.) the strategies elaborated here should work equally well on either platform, but you should note that minor variations on the information presented here may be apparent. Regardless, you should be able to use the information contained herein to achieve an equal command of Microsoft Word 2016 on your Mac as any Windows user with their respective machine.

CHAPTER 2

THE BASIC BASICS

MICROSOFT WORD 2016 is a type of program popularly known as a word processor, because its primary function is document creation through text input, editing, and formatting, using a graphic interface controlled both via keyboard and input devices such as a mouse or trackpad. While there are many programs to choose from to perform this seemingly simple function—many of which claim full Word compatibility—in practical use, it's difficult for any program to live up to Microsoft Word 2016's position as the default standard for creation of .doc and .docx files. Therefore, when it is required that deliverables be submitted in .doc or .docx format, the most direct solution for many users in order to ensure full compliance with Word's standard is simply to use Word for all document-creation needs.

Certainly it cannot be denied that while several programs directed specifically at professional writers have managed to attract a not insignificant core of devotees, when measured by sheer volume it's an inescapable fact that many more authors choose to stick with Word whether due to inertia, comfort, or lack of motivation to bother switching. And hey, for all its quirks and eccentricities, some of us even like the program! (Shh, don't tell anyone.)

In today's fast-paced world, it's easy to forget than only fifty years ago, to use a program with only a fraction of Word's current capabilities would have cost hundreds of thousands of dollars—and yet, even the attractive promise of free software and browser-based services now available nearly everywhere hasn't been enough to lure over five hundred million active users away from reliance on Word for their document processing needs, even in the rare occasion such free services do offer full-featured editing capabilities—so it's safe to say Word will likely be around for a while.

Word isn't perfect, however; the program has a number of quirks which can be confusing to beginning users. Many a Word neophyte has accidentally switched on one or the other of the program's many capabilities, only to wonder what in the world they just did to mess up their document—and how in the world they're ever going to switch it back!

The scope of this book won't allow us to cover all of Microsoft Word 2016's many eccentricities, of course—even when one considers the many fine books intended for advanced Word instruction, not one is truly comprehensive in documenting Word's capabilities and peculiarities. This ***Get to the Point!* Guide to Microsoft Word 2016** is no different, as our scope is limited to the most frequently used features and the most common problems encountered by novice to intermediate level Word users—but regardless, you should pick up more than enough to be confident in your abilities to solve nearly any problem that's likely to pop up in the course of your daily Word use— and you might just have some fun along the way. So let's get started!

CHAPTER 3

GET STARTED

THIS BOOK STARTS from the assumption you have a current, functioning and legal version of Microsoft Word 2016 already installed on your desktop or laptop machine. If this is not the case, I would direct you to the instructions provided by Microsoft or your vendor to install and register the software on the computer of your choice. (Of course, you also have the option of using the Web-based version of Word, which works much the same way as the desktop version, but for the sake of simplicity we will assume desktop-based Word use for the purposes of this book.)

This book also assumes you are familiar with the typical input devices common to contemporary computers, including the keyboard and mouse. You do not have to know how to type fluently by any means—I have sustained a professional technical writing career on shockingly poor touch-typing skills, I confess—but just as this book does not contain scope enough to teach you left from right, neither can we take the time and space necessary here to explain where the spacebar is and what it does. Neither will this book explain such features common to most or all computer programs such as scroll bars, nor basic activities such as resizing windows to fit your monitor. (If you are in fact a complete novice to computer use and in need of such instruction, I would refer you to any number of more appropriate books, or even hands-on instruction such as might be available at a local community college.)

As each new version of Word is built atop the structure established by prior versions, much of the advice in this book will apply to versions of Word previous to the current one; similarly, if you picked up this volume a while ago and the version has since changed, you will likely find much of this book still applicable—but I'd urge you to check for an updated version of the book to go along with the new Word for the most appropriate training.

As with all programs, Microsoft Word 2016 can be started in a number of ways, including navigating through Windows' familiar Start menu, typing 'Word' into the taskbar search box, clicking a taskbar icon, double-clicking desktop icons, or even configuring the program to autostart whenever the computer is turned on. None of these methods of opening the program is superior to any other or saves the average user any appreciable amount of time, so whichever method you're most comfortable with is perfectly fine.

Regardless of which manner you choose to start the program, if you start Word without opening a specific document, the Word **Start screen** will appear, presenting a list of recently used documents along with a selection of blank templates from which to choose. If you want to continue working on a previously created document, click its entry in the recently-used list, or click one of the templates to create a new document based on that template.

If you have time to kill and are so inclined, feel free to browse the provided templates to see if there's anything that appeals to you. Personally, I've never found any of Microsoft's templates to be of any use whatsoever—on the rare occasions I find a template necessary, I generally have to make it myself. If you or someone from your school or company has previously done this, you might find these personalized templates here (in which case they would obviously be much more likely to be relevant to you) but I find that even when organizations do have their own templates, rarely do they tend to be integrated within Word itself, instead typically provided as separate documents to be modified and reused at will.

Pro tip: Even if you do find an included default template that you think may prove useful, the catch-22 is that unless heavily modified or disguised, it will be instantly recognizable to your intended audience as a default MS Word template—and this can come across as lazy or unoriginal. For these and the abovementioned reasons, I generally advise eschewing the default templates, but your results may vary.

If you open Microsoft Word 2016 by opening a previously created document, you will not see the Word Start screen. The program also contains an option under **File→Options** allowing Word to always start with a blank document, bypassing the Start screen entirely. While admittedly I have rarely found the Start screen to be of use to me, I haven't felt the need to go to this extent—not yet, anyway. For one, I rarely open Word from an entirely 'square one' beginning point, as I almost always have a previous document or template to modify that contains much of the formatting already laid out properly, which allows me to simply save-as to a new document, delete out the previous content, and begin creating without spending five to ten minutes doing laborious formatting, eliminating another potential obstacle to creation. Secondly, while I fully admit that the effect induced in many by facing an entirely blank page is completely psychological, it's also very real: there is something so intrinsically intimidating about beginning from literally nothing that it can halt many would-be authors in their tracks, or at the very least send them scrambling for any of the thousands of potential distractions or procrastination aids this world offers us at any given moment. While I have heard some exult in the freedom and opportunity offered by the blank page, I have seen far more cowed into timidity by the daunting challenge it implicitly offers, and it is this latter tendency I have felt more often in my soul—or lack of same, as it can sometimes feel when writer's block threatens to strike. But in truth, no document truly starts from nothing, so even if you do find yourself beginning with an empty page, remember that everything you have done before has prepared you for that moment—presumably including reading this book!

For our purposes, let's assume you're starting with a blank document. At this point, you should see what appears to be a blank page, above which appears what's called the **ribbon**. The ribbon allows you to access most of Microsoft Word's commands and controls by navigating among several tabs, each of which is generally organized by function—although as we'll see, there is plenty of overlap in function between the various tabs. Don't worry; just as there are many ways to reach Rome, there are many routes through Word to reach the same destination. By the time we're finished, you'll have enough knowledge to get your writing done, one way or another!

Pro tip: Hover your cursor over any button or dropdown menu and a ScreenTip box containing a brief description of the button or menu's function will appear. Some of these ScreenTips allow you to press **F1** to bring up Office Help topics relating to that function.

I confess that I've personally never found Microsoft's included onboard help to be of much use. In most situations when you have a question about Word (that isn't answered by this book, obviously!) and you might consider consulting Office Help, unless you're already used to using the feature you'll probably find an answer and get back to work more quickly by searching for the answer to your specific query on Google than via Help—just make sure to use your best judgment and double-check that you only use reputable suggestions from qualified sources! Ironically, this will often be Microsoft's own documentation, but you'll almost always find that information faster by searching online than through Office Help's clunky Word interface—and this way, you can be assured you're receiving the most up-to-date solutions.

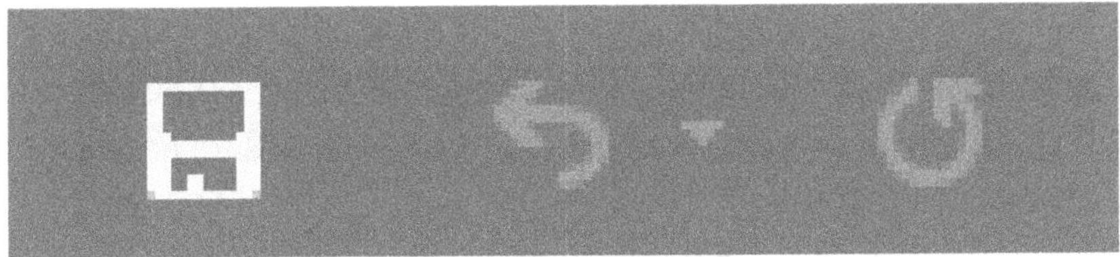

Atop the ribbon, across the top left side of the Microsoft Word window appear icons to **Save** the current document, **Undo** your most recent action, and to **Repeat** the most recent action. These buttons persist across every Word window, regardless of which tab is highlighted, although they are inactive and appear greyed out on the **File** tab, presumably to prevent the user from executing inadvertent content alterations while the content itself is hidden. (It's unknown why they bothered to grey out the **Save** button as well, though, especially considering the **File** tab boasts its own.) As Word retains the history of your actions in each editing session, if the undo button is clicked repeatedly, you can turn back the hands of time to when the document was first opened, undoing every change you've made.

As you step backwards through layers of undoing changes, you will notice a **Redo** button appears beside the **Undo** button, allowing you to step forward through your editing sessions and reimplement changes you've had second thoughts about reverting. Using these two controls, you can review the entire history of your session if you so desire—but note that once the document is saved and closed, the editing history for that session is cleared, so be careful you don't lose important changes you've already implemented unless you want to do them again, manually. If you think you might need to consult earlier versions of your document—and sometimes even if you don't—I suggest saving numbered and dated versions as a series of backups.

It only takes a moment at the beginning or end of each writing session, and you never know when a judicious backup might save you from having to repeat hours of tedious work. Worst case scenario, you'll never need to consult your old drafts and you maintain a complete record of your document's development process—fortunately, since the amount of space required to archive the typical Microsoft Word document is relatively small compared to the storage demands required for maintaining either physical paper archives or large digital files such as video, few users will ever find themselves in the position of needing to purchase additional storage solely for maintaining Word documents. (If anything, you might consider copying your entire Word document library to a cheap pocket flash drive or two in order to maintain additional backups in different locations for added security—something that can be accomplished today for a couple of dollars.)

Below the **Save**, **Undo**, and **Repeat** buttons appear the tabs of Word's **ribbon**. The tabs that appear on your particular installation of Microsoft Word 2016 can vary depending on whether optional plugins or add-ons have been installed, but in most cases the tabs should appear as follows:

- **File**
- **Home**
- **Insert**
- **Design**
- **Layout**
- **References**
- **Mailings**
- **Review**
- **View**
- **Tell Me...**
- **Share**

That might seem like a lot if you've never used Word before—and maybe even if you have, as it's common for users to become accustomed to using only a few familiar commands from the most easily accessed tabs and thereafter mentally 'blocking out' those features they're not used to, almost as if they were never there. (And really, if the user is never going to use them, does it matter?)

But no matter how comfortable you are with Word and its features, you'll soon see that once Word's many features are broken down by tab, it becomes much easier to bring a wider variety of Word's powerful tools to bear on each document you create, whether complex or simple—because once these commands become second nature, you'll find yourself moving at your natural pace, rather than allowing Word's perceived complexity and a series of less-than-ideal workarounds to limit your productivity.

We'll examine each tab in turn to see what controls and options each provides, learn what circumstances you might need to use them in, and finally we'll take a look at putting it all together to create a workflow that serves you in the simplest way possible to allow you to create your documents in the quickest, most efficient manner.

CHAPTER 4

FILE TAB

THE FILE TAB is the leftmost tab on the Word ribbon. Somewhat confusingly, File is the only tab which, when highlighted, obscures the current working document—and the live working area of the ribbon itself—in order to present an entirely new screen of properties, information, and commands.

For these reasons, it's easy to think of the **File** tab not as part of the ribbon proper—but instead, as a file access and properties area that is only relevant when you need to open, close, save, or print that document, or to gain information about the document itself (such as previous versions, size, and number of pages or words) but **not** to modify the content of the currently open document.

When considered in this light, the logic behind the unique organization of the **File** tab makes more sense: its dramatically different visual appearance serves as a cue that operations undertaken in the **File** screen function in an overall different manner than the other tabs, which by and large serve to edit and otherwise transform the content of a document.

When will you need to use the File tab and File screen?
For most users, the **File** tab and screen will be most frequently used for the following:

- **Saving a document as a new version**. The **File** screen does feature a 'Save' button and icon, of course— but as Word includes a standard **Save** icon above the ribbon that appears no matter which view is currently active, few will find this of much value. However, when working with long documents in particular, saving as a new version is recommended in order to preserve proper document control or merely to have a backup to which to revert in case of disaster. You can't have too many backups! If your version of Word has Adobe Acrobat plugins installed, you may also see a 'Save as Adobe PDF' option; you may also elect to save to .pdf via that standard 'Save as' dialog box. (Note that pdfs are intended primarily for final document delivery and are not a substitute for the standard .doc and .docx formats. Note also that 'Adobe PDF' is not necessarily superior or preferable to other types of PDF authoring, despite what Adobe would like you to believe.)

- **Creating a new document**. Assuming you didn't open Word in such a way as to show the Start screen, the File tab is where you'll come to create brand new, blank documents —you should be presented with the same choice of templates on either screen. Your new document will be created in .docx, the default XML-based format that has been standard ever since the previous .doc format was deprecated due to inconsistent compatibility with other word processing programs. If you'd prefer to work in .doc, simply select "save as" as shown above and reopen the newly created .doc—but unless you are required to submit in .doc format, be aware that .docx is generally superior and is nearly as widely accepted these days, so don't stick with .doc purely out of force of habit.

- **Printing or Exporting a document**. Somewhat self-explanatorily, while printing to dead tree pulp is no longer the primary use of Microsoft Word, the failure of the truly paperless office to supplant traditional working methods means printing to paper will remain necessary for some time to come. As more and more venues accept electronic submissions via .pdf, .doc and other formats, the need thankfully continues to decrease, but for the time being, when you need a hard copy of your document, the File menu's Print options will provide all the controls you need —and when you don't, the Export options allow you to create an electronic deliverable. In either case, you shouldn't need to adjust much, assuming your document was set up properly from the beginning—but keep an eye out for features offered by your particular printer, such as double-sided printing, collation, and orientation to ensure your printout will appear as expected before you hit 'Print'. Ink is expensive!

What else can you do with the File tab and File screen?
The File tab and screen also features the following (in my opinion) less-useful functions:

- The File screen does offer **Open** and **Close** buttons; though studies show the vast majority of users tend to open documents directly from their desktop directory and close them by clicking the 'x' in the top corner of the window, it's still helpful to remember where these functions are grouped. (Similarly, the File screen also offers an **Exit** button that I can't recall ever using.)
- **Share**. The intent here is that Microsoft Word 2016 function as the user's default program for not only word

processing, but also publishing to the web, email distribution, and even sending faxes! While it's great that Word offers such powerful capabilities, in reality I find most users have their own preferred solutions for each separate function. If you don't, you might find it worthwhile to research using Word to meet your specific needs—but in general, I think you'll find a dedicated program more likely to meet your needs unless your workplace or school is already using Share-integrated procedures. The rest of us can probably safely ignore Share entirely.

- **Access Advanced Options**. Although most techniques requiring use of advanced options lie outside the scope of this book, you may find it necessary to tweak one or another aspect of Word's behavior—optimizing the time between automatically saved recovery versions of your document to fit your computer's performance, for example. (More frequent autosaves are preferable to prevent data loss, but the interruption caused on older, slower machines can be irritating.) You might never need to use Options for anything at all, but should you discover that you do, the File tab is where you'll find the Options dialog—though I would caution you as a reader of this book to be absolutely certain to research any changes you intend to make to Options thoroughly. (And if you do want to change autosave frequency, click the File tab, click Options, click Save, and change the field labeled 'Save AutoRecover information every ___ minutes'.)

CHAPTER 5

PROTECTED VIEW

IF YOU'VE USED Microsoft Word 2016 to open document files sent to you via email or other online file transfer service, you've probably encountered **Protected View** already and had to click to make it go away, similar to the many security-intended nag dialogs Microsoft has embedded into Windows. Essentially, **Protected View** is a limited, read-only mode in which most editing tools are disabled, allowing the user to view the document but not much more. In this way, the user can get a look at the contents of a file without exposing their computer to problematic or malicious code that could harm the machine or otherwise compromise its security.

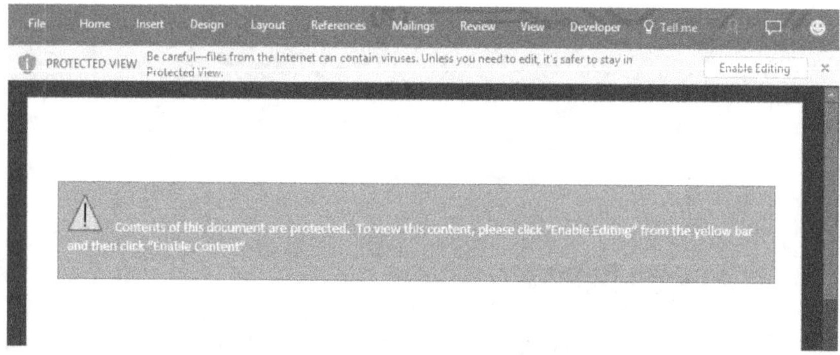

While well-intended, the problem with **Protected View**'s implementation is that it doesn't actually do much to screen potentially problematic files other than to alert the user and perform a simple file validation. Despite its firm wording, it doesn't scan for viruses, worms, or other types of malware within documents, instead placing the onus on you to determine whether the file is safe enough to open and edit—a decision that can easily bewilder a user who isn't entirely certain whether or not to trust a given file.

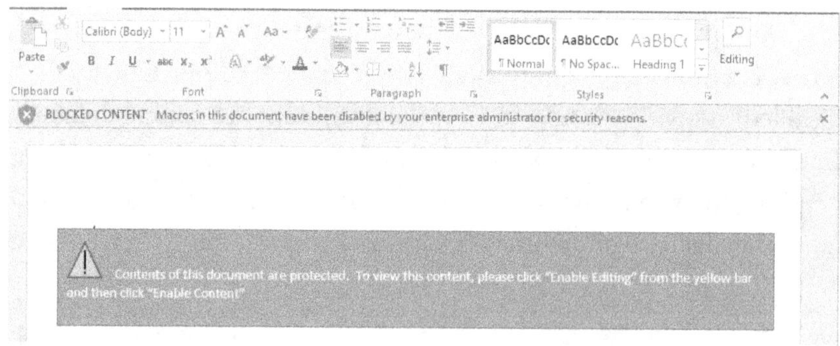

Fortunately, the risk from infected Word documents is relatively limited. Historically speaking, the overwhelming majority of malware found embedded within Word documents have been of the macro variety, and because few average Word users have any use for macros as a typical part of their workday, many organizations' security administrators have chosen to block macros as a matter of policy. For the most part, I recommend readers of this book avoid macros and documents containing them unless absolutely necessary, therefore limiting their exposure to macro malware with very little potential downside. On the rare occasion you do choose to enable macros, be absolutely certain of the source of the file before doing so—even if it appears to come from a legitimate source, it's worth confirming before exposing your machine to a potentially crippling macro virus. Many viruses replicate by infecting a user's stored contacts and emailing malicious attachments that appear to originate from known sources, so even if a dubious document seems to come from a trusted colleague, it may be worth reaching out to them via telephone to verify their email hasn't been compromised.

Ultimately, while **Protected View** can be useful to allow a user to get a peek at a document to determine its validity before opening for editing, Word should never be considered more than a final line of defense in your security policy, whether that of an entire organization or simply your own laptop. Before reaching the stage when you ever have to decide whether a file is legitimate or not, it should have already passed through a frequently updated virus protection program, a properly configured firewall, and a reliable malware and adbot scanner. While obviously the configuration of a complete security suite is beyond the scope of this book, I urge you not to rely solely on Word's included security tools to maintain the sanctity of your machine—a false sense of security often proves worse than none at all.

CHAPTER 6

HOME TAB

THE **HOME** TAB is aptly named: as location of the most frequently-used Word commands, it is the tab most likely to remain open at the top of your document for the longest amount of time while you are actively editing your document.

As a result, the Home tab contains a wide range of powerful functions which have been subdivided into five sections, left to right:

- **Clipboard**
- **Font**
- **Paragraph**
- **Styles**
- **Editing**

Because the Home tab contains so many powerful tools, this section is far and away the longest of any of the tab-specific chapters of this book. Don't worry! While it may seem lengthy at first, each of the Home tab's functions is in fact broken up quite logically, and taking note of the commands which are relevant to you is actually fairly straightforward—in fact, chances are you know most of them already. And don't despair, even if this seems initially overwhelming—later chapters in this book covering other tabs will be significantly shorter, corresponding to their much lower frequency of use. However, in the interest of expediency I will allow this much: if you're going to concentrate your effort in one section of this book to gain the greatest amount of directly useful, immediately applicable Microsoft Word 2016 knowledge in the shortest amount of time, here is where your effort should likely be expended.

At far left of the Home tab, **Clipboard** contains the most basic editing buttons, their functions self-evident from their names: **Cut** and **Paste**, which allow the user to cut selected text, retaining it in the clipboard until pasted in a new location or multiple locations. **Copy** copies the selected text to the clipboard without deleting it from its original location—extremely useful in many circumstances, such as when you've inserted a special character symbol that requires an elaborate keystroke combination or time-consuming menu naviga-tion to repeat. Much easier to copy the previous insertion and paste wherever you need it!

The **Format Painter** and **Paste Options** sections of the Clip-board section are advanced options dealing with text formatting that are likely to be of limited use to novice users. Briefly, Format Painter allows the user to duplicate the styles and formatting applied to a selection of text and apply that style formatting to additional text as desired; while Paste Options let the user copy and paste text with or without the formatting applied to the source text. In both cases, in the vast majority of circumstances most users will likely find it easier to apply formatting directly to their text—though I will allow that if you do find yourself neck-deep in a document requiring intensive, repeti-tive formatting, both Format Painter and Paste Options can be quite useful.

In the lower right corner of the Clipboard section, a small button allows toggling of the Clipboard sidebar, should you need to see text as it's copied to the clipboard or perform more advanced cut and paste functions using multiple items; in most cases, however, you won't need or want to see this sidebar and it should be kept closed.

The **Font** section of the Home tab contains controls that specify the appearance of the document's text; that is, the actual letters, numbers, and punctuation marks making up the words of your content. Microsoft Word 2016 ships with a number of default fonts, or typefaces, as shown on the font selection dropdown menu; the included selection will probably be sufficient to meet the needs of most users, but additional fonts can be added to your system relatively easily if necessary.

Regarding font choice I will not go into great detail here—as typesetting is a topic that could easily fill a book in itself—other than to say that if you're spending a lot of time choosing a font in Word, you're doing it wrong. Although Word has some design features, Word is not a full-featured design program by any means and should not be used as one. The primary intent of Word (and this guide) is to create communicative documents as quickly and easily as possible—and diverting yourself into endless dithering over font choice is time-wasting at best, utterly irrelevant or distracting at worst.

Unless directed otherwise—or you're designing a flyer for your neighborhood yard sale—in the vast majority of situations you should stick to eleven or twelve point text (the size number specified beside the font name) in a standard, readable font such as Times New Roman. If you have doubts, ask the intended audience, whether your boss, teacher or other authority what they would prefer—but regardless of the situation, don't get too clever with font tricks in Word. (I will note that Bookman Old Style does make a nice alternative to Times New Roman's serifed ubiquity, while I find Arial generally preferable to the default sans-serif font Calibri, but your results may vary.)

Below the font selection dropdown menu are buttons labeled **B**, *I*, and **U**, which respectively allow the user to make the selected type-face **boldfaced**, *italicized*, or underlined. (The Underline button also features a dropdown menu allowing choice of underline style.) Regarding when each of these is appropriate for use in your field we will leave to the reader, as such grammatical advice lies outside the scope of this book—leaving that aside only to say two things: one, that in most circumstances, italics are preferable to underlining, and two, that once you start emphasizing words with boldface and italics it's all too easy for a document to become a mishmash of garbled, overem-phasized text that seems to simultaneously glare and shout at the reader, insulting their intelligence by talking down to them and distracting them by robbing them of the chance to interpret the text for themselves. In most text, use emphases sparely if at all, and err on the side of caution.

Next to the Underline button and dropdown is the **abc** strikethrough button, allowing the user to format text as ~~strikethrough text~~. Formatting the previous sentence is the first time I've ever used that button, so you can probably safely ignore it unless you have a great need for strikethrough text in your field. (Who are these people, sometimes I wonder?). Beside the strikethrough button are $\mathbf{x_2}$ subscript and $\mathbf{x^2}$ superscript buttons, of most use to those in math and science-related fields in which chemical formulas, ordinal indicators and the like often use subscripts and superscripts frequently. If you are engaged in such a pursuit, you probably know how likely you are to need sub- and superscripts; if so, take note of these buttons now, but most will use them rarely if at all.

The Font section also contains buttons to nudge font size up or down, as well as a dropdown menu to change sentence case of selected text between ALL CAPS, lowercase, Capitalize Each Word, or Sentence case, and a button to clear formatting from the selected text. I don't think I've ever used any of these regularly, though I admit in profes-sional use I switch sentence case frequently using the Shift+F3 keyboard combination. However, most users will not need to change sentence case often enough to justify either memorizing that keystroke combination nor the location of this dropdown menu—but if you do, here it is.

Similarly included are tools for Text Effects, allowing you to use letters that are outlined, reflected, or seem to glow. Again, I feel trying to use Word in this manner is counter to its strengths—as a graphics design program, Word makes a great word processor. The highlighting option and ability to change the text color are slightly more likely to come in actually useful in legitimate use, particularly for users who might be used to applying liberal amounts of high-lighter pens to their paper drafts or study materials—but I would caution you against using these options too liberally in any finalized document.

In the lower right corner of the Font section, a small button allows you to bring up the Font dialog box. The Font dialog box can indeed be useful, though I tend to only invoke it after right-clicking on selected text and choosing **Font…** to apply formatting to the selected text, so invoking the Font dialog by itself without having text selected frankly seems less than advantageous.

Next to the Font section of the Home tab is the **Paragraph** section, where formatting expands from the type, shape, and style of the letters and numbers used to make up your document to the space between lines, how those lines are arranged, and how they appear. If you want your text arranged with multilevel indentations like a tradi-tional outline, as a bulleted or numbered list, or sorted in alphabetical order, the Paragraph section allows you to quickly format selected text using a number of preselected bullets, styles, and formats. In all cases, the provided selection should be more than enough to cover nearly any relevant use, and the result will almost always appear more professional than if you had attempted to do it by hand.

As a professional technical writer, one of the most painful mistakes I see time and again from novice users is painstakingly and timeconsumingly attempting to format numbered or alphabetical lists manually, entering each by hand—only for them to have to renumber the entire list each time an entry is inserted. People—this is what computers were created for! When you need a numbered or alphabetized list, always let the machine do the work for you—simply enter the text without the intended numbering or lettering, select the text to be formatted, and press the corresponding button or dropdown menu to either apply the default style or select from a number of other appropriate choices.

One commonly cited frustration with Word is a perceived inability to control the program's automatic formatting as one types—for instance, entering the number '1' followed by a space leads Word to assume the user is beginning a numbered list, and it will format the text accordingly. It's worth noting that this automatic formatting is always registered as an undoable action, so that whenever Word 'helpfully' formats your text in a manner you didn't want, just hit Undo once and it will revert to your original formatting as typed. If you find AutoCorrect formatting continually causing slowdowns in your workflow, you can navigate to **File → Options → Proofing** and click **AutoCorrect Options** to change how Word will **Auto-Format** your text, but I'd be leery of throwing the baby out with the bathwater, so to speak—generally speaking, AutoFormat is more useful than not, as long as you know how to get rid of its effects easily when unwanted.

Paragraph alignment is also controlled here, via four buttons arranged from left to right: **Align Text Left**, **Center**, **Align Text Right**, and **Justify**. In nearly all professional capacities, left alignment is the appropriate choice—and like fancy text effects, aligning complex graphic elements is best done in programs other than Word. However, titles are often centered, so this function can come in handy in such cases. Justify adjusts the spacing between letters so as to create an even margin along both sides of the page, rather than a straight left side and a ragged right side; in most cases left alignment should be used, as justified text can have an unprofessional, artificial appearance, but if the situation so demands, here is where it can be accomplished.

The Paragraph section of the Home tab is also host to one of Word's features that is most frequently misunderstood by novice users: the ability to show and hide formatting marks. These marks are vital to professional users such as myself, and can be quite useful even to intermediate-level Word users, but they often serve to confuse others when suddenly, text that previously had appeared normal suddenly has dots between every word and marks at the end of every paragraph! Many a user has caught their breath, worried they've irretrievably ruined their document, wondering if they have a backup without dots they can revert to—only to find those dots now cover even their saved backups!

Fret not: formatting marks exist purely within the background of your document, intended to be brought to the surface only to shape its content in the most efficient manner, and will be invisible when your document is printed or otherwise published. If all you ever use is a fairly standard layout or unmodified template, you may never need to see the formatting marks in your own documents—but whether you do or not, it's easy enough to turn them on and off at will: towards the center of the Home tab ribbon on the Paragraph group, a large button labeled with a ¶ paragraph mark serves to make the formatting marks visible or invisible while editing. When depressed, the button is illuminated to indicate invisible formatting marks have been made visible—though in all fairness, this should be fairly obvious in all but the blankest of documents.

I'll spare you the hacky jokes about the **Styles** section appearing in your local newspaper and simply note that this section contains its own browser allowing you to peruse currently defined styles as they apply to the document you're currently working on. Please note that when you hover the mouse pointer over a particular style in the

Styles browser, the current section of text being worked on will shift to that style to preview how that style would appear within the document—but that style is only applied to the text once you click the style. Also note that while styles can be very helpful in long, complicated professional documents, you may not necessarily find much use for them in your typical course of work—or you may be required to use specific, predefined styles other than those already defined within Word. If this is the case, don't feel obligated to use the Styles browser until you feel comfortable doing so, as you're unlikely to save a significant amount of time unless the document in question requires frequent, repetitive, or complicated style formatting.

The **Editing** section contains some of Word's most powerful tools: **Find**, **Replace**, and **Select**. Although I couldn't get through my daily technical writing work without using these commands —**Replace** in particular—I advise caution to novices when using these potent tools.

Find is fairly benign, allowing the befuddled user to locate his or her bearings within the forest of a lengthy, disorganized draft—yet when paired with its partner replace, the potential for wreaking havoc upon a document is almost incalculable. For this reason, I suggest a high degree of caution before executing any Find and Replace command, including saving a separate backup draft beforehand in case you find yourself needing to revert the damage you've inadvertently caused!

To get an idea of the problems a poorly-considered Find/Replace action can cause, consider this example: say you've drafted a set of procedures for your company's information technology department, and to save yourself time while writing, you type each instance of 'information technology' as simply 'IT', intending to execute a Find/Replace action when the text is finished to change each occurrence of 'IT' to 'information technology'.

Great idea! Unfortunately, while Replace is a powerful tool, it's not great at knowing what you meant—it requires very specific formatting and knowledge of its options. In our example, if you failed to select 'Match case', it would change every instance of the word 'it' to 'information technology'—and if you failed to put spaces before and after 'IT' in the Find box, it would also change every occurrence of the letters 'i' and 't' together in the middle of words as well. So 'withdraw' could become 'winformation technologyhdraw', 'legitimate' could become 'leginformation technologyimate', and so forth. I trust you can easily envision the mess this would make of your hard work in no time!

Select, like Find, seems relatively harmless on its own—the danger here is that you may not be completely aware of exactly what has been selected, and inadvertently misapply unintended modifications to sections of text that can be difficult to revert.

I don't mean to scare you off these tools, but I can't emphasize enough the necessity to consider carefully every action you take with the Editing tools—for I can tell you from all too painful personal experience just how easy it is to make a lot of work for yourself with Word when trying to save yourself a little. Just make sure to back up regularly, and if the result doesn't look like you expected, be sure to hit that undo button before you hit save! (And if you've followed the advice given above, you should be able to revert to an earlier draft in any case...but sometimes such lessons have to be learned the hard way.)

CHAPTER 7

INSERT TAB

IF YOU'RE a complete novice to using Word, I sympathize—at this point, your head is probably swimming from the variety of controls featured on the Home tab alone!

Fortunately, the number and range of tools included on the **Insert** tab is nowhere near as intensive as the Home tab. In fact, as we'll see, compared to the Home tab, most of the other tabs are generally quite straightforward and function-directed, rather than combining a wide range of tools on one page the way the Home tab does. So if your head is already aching, don't worry—you've done most of the hard work already, and it only gets easier from here.

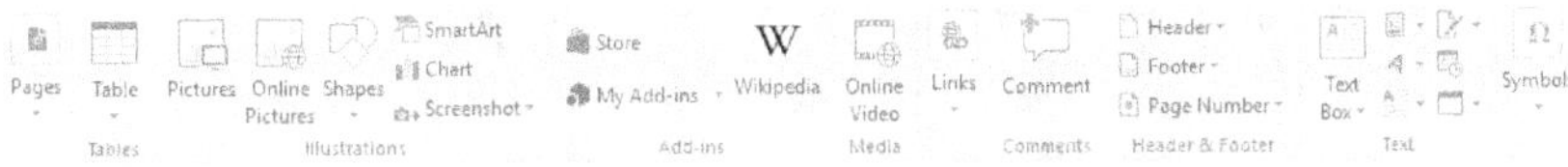

Unfortunately, I feel the Insert tab is somewhat poorly named for its function; though I understand the intent, 'Insert' is a somewhat incomplete description of the tools gathered there. You may find it easier to think of the Insert tab as 'Insert Special Features', as this is closer to how most users will interact with the Insert tab tools. I say this because for the most part, the Insert tab tools deal with additions to a document other than the text itself, such as cover pages, images, and overall document formatting such as page numbering, headers and footers. Even when Insert tools act upon the text itself, such as the Equation and Symbol tools, they are adding elements generally considered unusual to the usual text content, such that they do not appear on any standard keyboards.

At left, the **Pages** section contains a browser featuring a number of cover page designs that are subject to the same caveats previously applied to Microsoft's included templates—use them if you like, but in my experience virtually no one does in any professional capacity. When I need a cover page, I design it myself, always erring on the side of simplicity, and most organizations tend to have their own preferred choices as well. Similarly, I've never found a use for Pages' insert **Blank Page** function, preferring to manually insert page breaks in the rare circumstances I require a blank page. Fortunately, the insert **Page Break** button also appears here; I suggest using it in between chapters—a novice will tend to simply hit Enter repeatedly until they reach the next page, but this can give your document an amateurish appearance and throw your pagination off badly as further edits are made.

Beside pages is **Tables**, a powerful and useful tool for adding tables to your document—though somewhat confusingly, not tables of contents or figures, which fall under the References tab. The Table dialog does contain a number of simple tools allowing you to define your table's appearance either by entering number of rows and columns (**Insert Table...**), by drawing it directly into your document (**Draw Table**), by inserting a predefined table from a set of templates (**Quick Tables**), or by inserting a Microsoft Excel spreadsheet. Which option you'll want to use depends heavily on what type of table you need, what it will be used for, and your level of comfort with the various table-drawing tools; I recommend keeping your table exactly as complex as it needs to be to convey the necessary information, and no more—while Word's tools are more than sufficient to create nearly any type of table required, going much beyond that is stretching into the realm of graphic design, at which Word is far from the best solution.

Similarly, the next set of tools on the Insert tab should be used with caution, as **Illustrations** truly fall outside Word's primary set of strengths.

Here is where you will go to insert images such as the screenshot above, placed by clicking **Picture** and navigating to the file's location within my desktop directory structure. While this is simple enough, regarding the remaining tools under Illustrations—**Online Pictures** (formerly **Clip Art**), **Shapes**, **SmartArt**, **Chart**, and **Screenshot**, I will say only that when I have a need for any of the functions these tools cover, I don't use Word and I don't generally recommend that others do either. Any number of tools from Visio to free, open source alternatives offer far superior options for chart and flowchart creation, and I quite frankly can't imagine why anyone would want to take screenshots of another program through Word. If you do have a one-time need for a very simple chart, image, or illustration, or you're already familiar with their use and have already integrated them into your daily workflow in a useful way (doubtful, if you're reading this book), you might find these tools useful, but even in such cases I would generally recommend investigating other solutions before resorting to Word's inferior options.

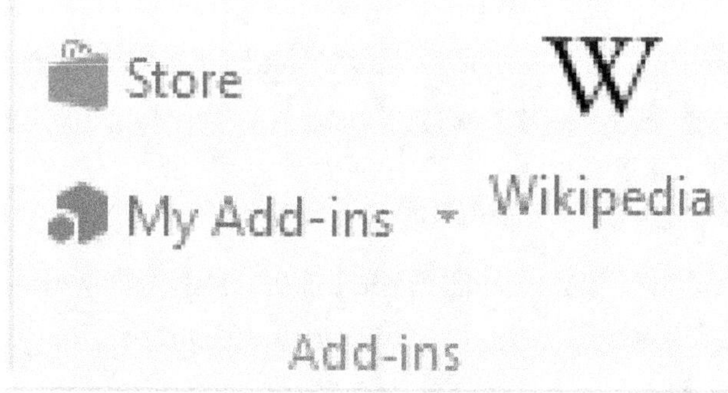

Beside Illustrations is a section for any **Add-ins** with which you've personalized your version of Word, as well as a link to find the **Store** where such add-ins can be purchased and downloaded, some for free. As the scope of this book doesn't allow us to detail the wide variety of add-ins available and what they do, I will say only that there is an argument to be made for keeping your installation of Word operating as smoothly and cleanly as possible by eschewing unnecessary add-ins, removing the potential for workflow-disrupting conflicts and interference. Should you find an add-in you think will facilitate your workday, investigate thoroughly and do your due diligence to ensure the add-in's creator intends it for the use to which you intend to put it; if not, you may be in for more frustration or disappointment than if you'd simply done it yourself without the add-in's well-intended help.

Regarding the **Online Video Media** section I will say merely this: don't. Unless you have been specifically requested to do so, please— just don't. I can appreciate Microsoft's attempts to keep the program current with technological developments, but unless you have a specific need for inserting online video into a document and for doing that from within Microsoft Word, it's a bad idea: online video is liable to change or vanish without notice, so the end experience for your ultimate reader may not remotely resemble your intentions. And even if you're able to dodge such problems, you can't control the range of devices your document might be opened on, many of which may not even have the capability necessary to render video. Finally, you do your document little service by inserting such blatant distractions—over-adornment is often taken as a sure sign of desperation. (And if your project truly requires a significant amount of video content, perhaps it would be better executed as a video, not a Word document.)

Much more useful is the **Links** section, which will allow you to add a dynamic link to whatever online content you might want to reference, without actually intrusively inserting that content into your document. Generally, Word 2016 is configured to automatically parse URLs written in standard formats with leading 'www.' or http://' prefixes, but using these tools you can control every aspect of how those links appear, whether the URLs appear in full (http://example.com) or concealed behind linking display text (example). Just as important, selecting hyperlinked text and opening the **Hyperlink** dialog will allow you to remove hyperlink metadata, so that you can include a URL like http://example.com without it also functioning as a link to that location. (Of course, these functions can also be accomplished by selecting the text to be linked, right-clicking, and selecting **Hyperlink...** to open the Hyperlink dialog.)

As I tend to think of bookmarks as tools to keep one's place in a finished book or document, I've never found internal document bookmarks to be of much use in document creation, preferring to place them manually or derive them from heading formatting when creating a pdf document. I have seen them used occasionally by document authors who work from a highly hierarchical standpoint and need to jump from place to place within a draft frequently, but even in such cases I've been highly dubious whether much time was saved in the process of creating, maintaining, and later removing said bookmarks, particularly when compared with the increase in productivity generally seen when using tools such as multiple windows or split-screen views as opposed to jumping around frequently.

If you use do use Word bookmarks regularly, Links is where the **Bookmark** tool can be found: to use, simply place the cursor where you'd like the bookmark to appear, click the **Bookmark** tool, and type a name for the bookmark. You can navigate among the bookmarks you've placed via the **Find and Replace** dialog, brought up by pressing **Replace** on the **Home** tab. Once the dialog box appears, click the **Go To** tab and select **Bookmark** under **Go to what:**, then choose the bookmark you'd like to jump to. As user-defined bookmarks do not appear in Word's handy **Navigation Pane**, (see View tab) this lengthy, click-intensive process for navigating among bookmarks is one of the primary obstacles to its usefulness, I'm afraid; frankly, if you find yourself with a job complex enough that you need bookmarks simply to maintain control of its organization, you have my sympathy.

Significantly more useful is the **Cross-reference** dialog which can also be summoned from the **Links** section. For users who have to create lengthy technical documents containing many tables, figures, or headings, the ability to create dynamic references to those items can be an immense timesaver. Say, for example, a document contains forty tables, each of which is referred to within the text by its numbered heading—and then an additional table is inserted at the beginning of the text. If the user is working manually, each of those subsequent table headings and references would have to be laboriously updated by hand, all the while praying that a second table insertion wouldn't necessitate repeating the whole process over again!

Instead, to create a dynamic cross-reference that can update seamlessly with any future new additions to your text, place the cursor where the reference should appear in the text, press **Cross-reference** to bring up the **Cross-reference** dialog, select the type of item to be referenced (such as table, figure, numbered heading, and so forth), choose how the reference should appear, and click Insert. Later, if the reference needs to be updated, simply select the reference, right-click, and choose **Update Field**; alternately, all fields within a document can be updated at once by selecting all text within a document and pressing **F9**.

The **Insert** tab contains a section pertaining to inserting **Comments** into your document; we will cover this in more detail later under the **Review** tab, which offers more extensive comment-handling features (and where **Comments** should likely have solely remained, as in previous versions of Word.)

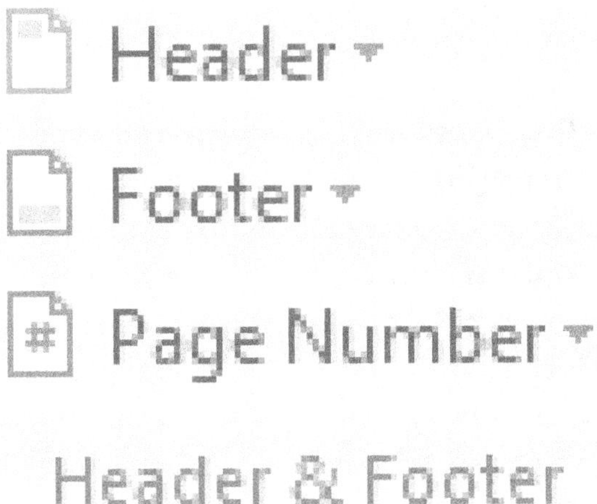

The **Header & Footer** section allows you to quickly and easily create headers, footers, and page numbers in the margins of your document to give it a more professional look. If your organization has defined standards or templates you may be limited in your choices, but the options Word offers range all the way from the standard and sober to the silly and overly busy. Unless you have concrete reasons for doing so, I'd recommend either sticking to the most basic of options or switching to a design-oriented program if you find yourself wanting to get ambitious with your page design.

Similarly, the **Text** box options edge into the realm of document layout and publishing just enough to be dangerous. Adding flourishes like **Drop Caps**, a spot quote in a **Text Box**, and special effect lettering with **WordArt** can look highly attractive when applied by a skilled typesetter, but can get confusing, amateurish, and problematic when used indiscriminately, and are rarely appropriate in any professional or academic capacity. Additionally, although its features allow a certain amount of layout and design to facilitate straightforward document creation, Word is far from a professional publishing solution and should not be used as such. If you'd care to use the **Text** section's **Signature Line** tool to create a standard signoff, or insert the current **Date and Time** in a number of standard formats with one click, those functions can be accomplished here.

Finally, the **Insert** tab's **Symbol** and **Equation** tools allow the relatively easy insertion of nonstandard symbols that would otherwise require many difficult workarounds or external tools to handle. Equations can be inserted as given from a selection of preinstalled common formulas, edited to conform to your needs, or created from scratch; if you believe you're likely to need to insert a significant number of equations into your documents I'd suggest taking an afternoon to play around with the **Equation** tools, familiarizing yourself with its capabilities, but the rest of us can probably skip it safely.

Symbol insertion, conversely, is nearly self-explanatory: pressing the **Symbol** button brings up a gallery of most commonly-used symbols; if the symbol you need isn't there (for whatever reason, mine never seem to be), click **More Symbols...** to bring up a comprehensive list of whatever symbols and special characters are associated with the current font being used within the document.

Pro tip: I generally find each document only requires one or two of these special symbol characters, each of which is a bit of a pain to insert through the Symbol dialog every time you need to use it—but not enough of a pain to bother learning its corresponding keystroke combination. Instead, after a symbol has been inserted once, I copy and paste from that location to wherever I need that symbol within the document, saving time, effort, and unnecessary additional strain on my clicking finger!

CHAPTER 8

DON'T MEMORIZE KEYBOARD 'SHORTCUTS' (EXCEPT THESE FOUR)

IF YOU'VE LOOKED through other books about Microsoft Word or read lists of Word tips and tricks online, you've undoubtedly encountered long, confusing lists of keyboard shortcuts used for every conceivable purpose. Whether to navigate within a document, insert special characters, execute formatting and layout, or simply copy and paste, Word features a dizzying array of keyboard shortcuts allowing the user to hypothetically save time and mouseclicks. And for some writers—like, say, the authors of comprehensive instructional books about Microsoft Word—memorizing dozens of keyboard shortcuts may be an efficient use of their time and energy.

However, when looked at from the perspective of the average user, this mindset doesn't make much sense. How many hours do you think you'd have to invest to memorize all of the dozens (if not hundreds) of commands necessary for every possible problem you might encounter? And once you've done so, how long do you think it'd take you before you actually have a reason to put that knowledge to use if you weren't just itching for a chance to do so? Long enough, perhaps, for you to forget most of what you'd learned?

At the beginning of my writing career I assumed over time I'd eventually come to use most of the keystroke commands for different purposes and retain them for future use, but like any foreign language, when vocabulary is not used consistently it tends to be forgotten quickly—for good reason, I say! It's already all too easy to clutter up your mind with irrelevant information by convincing yourself you'll be saving time in the future, when chances are you'll be much better off spending that time actually writing instead. The world has enough distractions to pull you away from writing already —don't let Word itself become an impediment to your work. (If you do find this to be a consistent problem for you, several providers do offer stripped-down word processors with heavily simplified interfaces to offer the least amount of distraction possible, but I suspect the dozens of other potential distractions even the most basic of computers or phones currently offer to be more problematic than any word processor could ever be.)

Frankly, Word makes most functions more easily accessible and controllable via menus and more modern interfaces than the archaic keystroke commands, so trust me when I tell you to forget them with impunity—in the overwhelming majority of cases, the time you might save just doesn't add up.

Of course, there are specific exceptions where keyboard shortcuts might well save you time—say, for example, a financial reporter who often writes about international issues would probably do well to memorize the Ctrl+Alt+E keystroke command to insert the € Euro symbol. But the rest of us, well—just ask yourself how often you really need to insert that symbol. Would the time it takes to recall or research that keystroke really be any faster than clicking Insert, then Symbol to find the one special character you actually need in that specific case? Chances are, probably not.

The truth is, in over two decades as a professional technical writer I've managed to not only get by, but excel in my chosen field with only a handful of keystroke shortcuts—and by 'a handful', I mean approximately seven:

- **copy (Ctrl+C)**
- **paste (Ctrl+V)**
- **undo (Ctrl+Z)**
- **redo (Ctrl+Y)**
- **change case (Shift+F3)**
- **insert soft return (Shift+Enter)**
- **insert page break (Ctrl+Enter)**

And remember, this is what I need for addressing the demands of a fulltime technical writing career, including creating documents for behemoth clients including the US Navy and Hewlett-Packard. Most people can probably get by without the last three, although despite my seemingly severe anti-keyboard shortcut stance I confess I'd find it hard to get through the workday without the first four.

Your results may vary, of course, but I'd suggest **Ctrl+C**, **Ctrl+V**, **Ctrl+Z**, & **Ctrl+Y** are the four shortcuts that will actually lead to an increase in your productivity—try them and see!

Everything else I need to do I do via the ribbon, and on the off-chance I find myself needing to use a specific keyboard shortcut, I simply search for it online, remember it for the course of working on that particular document, and then forget it immediately afterwards. The other special secret trick to remember about symbols is that you can copy and paste them just like any other characters—so once you manage to insert one instance of a particular character, whenever you need it again you'll find it's often faster to just scroll back up, copy it from wherever you first placed it and then paste it into its new location or locations, rather than to use the Symbol dialog every time.

CHAPTER 9

DESIGN TAB

THE **DESIGN** TAB (formerly part of 'Page Layout' in previous versions of Word) allows a variety of preinstalled themes—consisting of groups of coordinated colors, fonts, and styles—to be applied to control the overall visual impact of your document, as well as to change the appearance of the 'paper' that serves as the background of your document.

As this book has made clear multiple times, Word's strength as a program does not lie in its design or layout capabilities, and several tools on the **Design** tab duplicate functions more readily accessible elsewhere with a finer degree of control. And generally speaking, getting too creative with a document by changing page color or adding decorative borders within Word is often a wrongheaded idea by default, if not entirely a waste of time and effort. Therefore, it is entirely likely many users will not have much, if any need to use the

Design tab—but we will detail the options offered in case one proves useful.

Themes as presented on Word's **Design** tab control the overall appearance of a document similarly to templates; in fact, each theme is basically a template for how text should appear and behave within that document. Controls for **Colors** and **Fonts** appear here along with **Paragraph Spacing**, unfortunately without much to differentiate them from the similarly-named tools located on the **Home** tab. The **Design Color** and **Font** controls ostensibly function to control those aspects within the document's overall theme, allowing you to cycle through a variety of different styles and effects rapidly in order to define the overall appearance of your document.

While this can be an attractive option for a novice who fancies him- or herself an amateur graphic designer, in practice it can result in hours of wasted time and a less attractive or communicative end result. If you'd like to use **Themes** to control the overall look of your document, fine—just be sure to pick an appropriate choice and move forward, without succumbing to the temptation to tweak your choice endlessly as the document progresses. Chances are, should they notice at all, your intended audience will be annoyed by your attempts at distracting graphic design; you're better off concentrating your time and effort on the content of your text, or using a proper layout and design program to handle graphic elements, if you're serious about controlling the minutiae of your document's visual appeal.

In all fairness, it's not too difficult to imagine a situation where one might want to use the **Design** tab's **Watermark** feature within the **Page Background** section, even in a professional capacity; many government agencies and other bureaucratic organizations relish embedding their seals and logos into the background of every piece of communication, whether printed on official letterhead or not, and on many an occasion a glaring DRAFT, SAMPLE, or CONFIDENTIAL background watermark has prevented misuse of such information. The **Watermark** tool features preconfigured templates to insert just such warnings along with several others, as well as the controls to define a **Custom Watermark…**, including text content and appearance or to use a linked image file—the option you'd use for a seal or logo. While Adobe Acrobat's watermarking features are arguably more comprehensive and flexible—I personally tend toward watermarking deliverables far more often this way than via Word—watermarking in Word is painless and straightforward for the most part, as is the procedure should you need to **Remove Watermark**, which can also be accomplished here.

The **Page Background** section's remaining tools, **Page Color** and **Page Borders**, should probably be left alone unless you have specific need to change these items within Word or you happen to be using the program to throw together a five-minute flyer for a neighborhood garage sale. Uncontextural alterations to page color in Word documents are jarring and unwelcomed by most audiences, and design elements such as borders should generally be confined to cover pages rather than applied indiscriminately.

CHAPTER 10

LAYOUT TAB

THE **LAYOUT** TAB contains the remaining functions from what was the 'Page Layout' tab in previous versions of Word, controlling overall layout and design elements which can be applied either to the entire document or only to certain sections, specifying how text should interact with graphic elements, and defining margins, page orientation, and other text effects.

It's unclear what improved functionality or advantage Microsoft imagined would be conveyed by splitting Page Layout into **Design** and **Layout**—many would argue the terms are virtually synonymous in the context of working with Word—but the end result is that **Layout** contains significantly more useful tools than its counterpart.

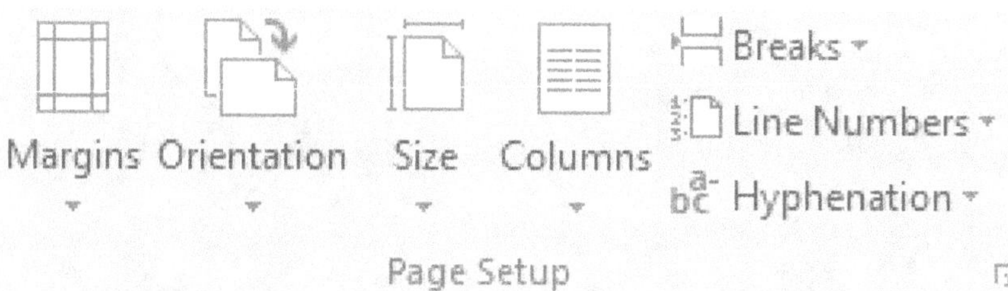

Adjusting **Margins** within a Word document is an old favorite among high school and undergraduate students attempting to give their document the appearance of greater heft than it deserves, artificially lengthening pagecount by using **Wide** margins rather than the more generally acceptable **Normal** or **Moderate** margins, each of which can be selected beneath the **Margins** button along with a number of other popular choices, as well as the option to define custom margins. **Narrow** margins can be useful for fitting a large amount of information on a single sheet of paper for personal use, but I wouldn't recommend it for most professional or academic documents.

I highly suggest most users stick with the **Normal**, **Moderate**, or **Default** margins for the overwhelming majority of projects, as quirky margins can quickly lend a document an amateurish appearance—and widespread knowledge of the old students' trick may lead some readers to suspect an author who plays with their margins may also be trying to deceive them in other ways. (Of course, if you're working with nonstandard paper sizes, unusual or custom margins may prove necessary, but it's unlikely you'll be doing so from within Word or in the course of producing any academic or business documentation.)

The controls in the **Paragraph** section fine-tune the appearance of your document's paragraph formatting, including precise amount of indenting either from the right or left, spacing before and after paragraphs, and the like. Assuming you've been reading this book in order, you may be scratching your head—didn't the **Home** tab also feature a Paragraph section? (Yes.) And can't the Paragraph dialog be summoned at any time by right-clicking and selecting Paragraph to fine-tune your paragraph layout choices? (Again, yes.)

So what advantages does this second, seemingly superfluous **Paragraph** tab offer? I'm afraid the answer is none, other than saving you the click back to the Home tab if you're already performing significant formatting changes to your document using the Layout tab's other tools. For this reason, I suggest most users consider the Home tab's Paragraph section as Word's primary paragraph formatting tool, and relegate the Layout section's redundant tools to occasional use when applicable.

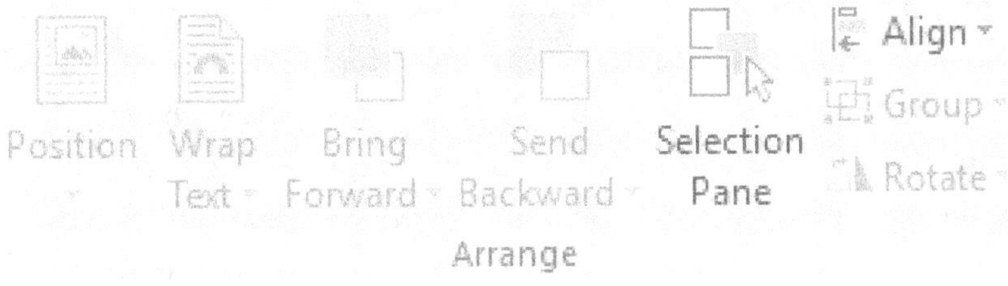

The **Arrange** section relates to the composition of images and other special features within your document, where they appear on the page, how they will interact with the text and with each other. In most cases when you're placing an image into a document, a simple **In Line with Text** position will do (as in this text), but the requirements of your organization's style guide or standard formatting may dictate otherwise. If so, **Position** will allow you to place images on a page with a wide range of layout options, including left, right, center, top and bottom alignments, and images can be layered using **Bring Forward** and **Send Backward** to control which pictures appear 'closer' to the reader.

Wrap Text allows you to control how text behaves when it is near pictures you've placed within a document. Again, in most cases the default **In Line with Text** option will suffice to meet your needs, but text can also run on top of images, through them, or even behind them! Again, in most cases I would advise against trying to get too fancy with Word's layout features—the type of intense graphic design work required to get ambitious layouts to work properly is best performed with design- and layout- specific programs, not a word processor.

Still, Word's capabilities should be more than enough to accomplish most of what one might choose to do with images in the typical document—and if not, remember this **Pro Tip**: often when only a page or two out of a lengthy document requires unique image arrangement, design, or layout, it's far more efficient to create those pages in more appropriate programs than Word then drop them into the completed deliverable than to spend the time trying to force Word to act against its nature. Simply put, some complex layout and design choices cannot be achieved within Word, and it's a fool's errand to try—but for the most part, I suspect you'll find Word more than sufficient to meet your needs, assuming you aren't an advanced student of the typographical arts.

CHAPTER 11

REFERENCES TAB

HAVE you recently become enamored of the work of David Foster Wallace and want to know how you, too, can insert copious footnotes, endnotes, and the like into your writing? I would caution you against it, as such devices are generally best left to those with the mastery to employ them—but if you insist, then the **References** tab is where you'll need to be.

I exaggerate slightly, of course—particularly in academic, business, and technical writing, there are plenty of occasions where use of footnotes is perfectly legitimate, and even necessary. Yet even here, it's often worth considering the loss in readability and linear clarity incurred by sending the reader off on a wild goose chase to a completely separate section of a document, expecting them to return to their original place and resuming as if no disruption had occurred. So unless you are authoring a 'Choose Your Own Adventure' type of book with multiple endings or deliberately trying to evoke the overwrought style of a tortured literary genius, I suggest such devices should be employed with care, and only when necessary.

Judiciously employed, the tools offered on the **References** tab can in fact add clarity and navigability to your document. Nearly any document of a certain length can benefit from the addition of a well-formatted table of contents, and the many preconfigured options offered by Word's **Table of Contents** tools should suffice for nearly any document.

Note that once placed, a Word table of contents will not automatically update as you continue to add to and edit that document. As one tends to continuously modify a document while it's actively being created, this is an easy fact to forget, so if you choose to place your table of contents before your document is completely finished, you must remember to right-click anywhere on your table and select 'Update Field' to ensure each of your table's references points to the proper location, rather than some random place where the information your reader is looking for used to be. When you update tables of contents (routinely referred to as TOCs in professional circles) you will generally be offered the option to 'Update page numbers only' or to 'Update entire table'; unless you are editing an exceptionally long document on an exceptionally slow computer, it's difficult to imagine many circumstances in which updating only the page numbers would save most users any appreciable amount of time, so I suggest you always default to 'Update entire table.' (As shown below, 'Update Table' also appears as an option in the Table of Contents section.)

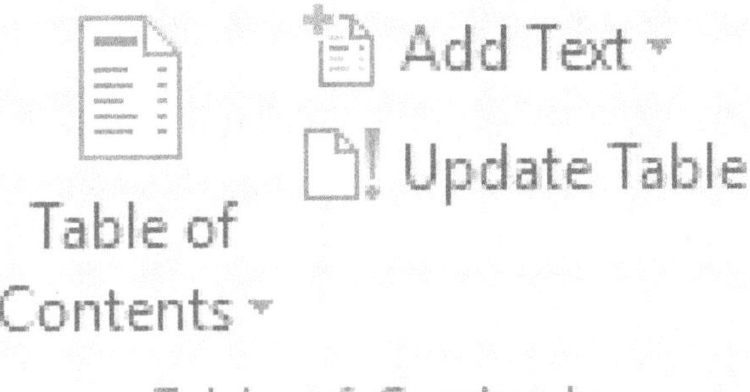

Generally, TOCs are built automatically by parsing the heading formatting placed within a document as shown within the samples in the TOC gallery, so if you have sections of your document set off properly with headings, constructing a useful, efficient table of contents can be as easy as selecting a TOC style, inserting it, and remembering to update it before you're finished. If not, well...you may be in for a long session of inserting headings in the correct locations and modifying your content to conform to proper formatting. This isn't as difficult as it might sound, but it is inarguable that any time spent fussing with internal document formatting is time not spent creating or editing the actual content of that document. For that and other reasons, I suggest that in most cases readers should probably stick within the offered gallery of TOC styles until they feel confident to modify a document's formatting codes without derailing a potentially productive work session into a nightmare of obsessive tweaking.

By default, your new table of contents listing contains hyperlink functionality, allowing you to press Ctrl + click to jump to the location listed, so your TOC can assist you while creating long documents by allowing you to jump from one section to another quickly and easily—for example, I can tell you honestly that I used this document's TOC nearly every single day to navigate among this book's many sections while creating it. In addition to contents, tables can also be built to index headings, equations, authorities (or sources), or even other tables, so depending on your document's requirements, the TOC tool is flexible enough to handle many an index without difficulty and far more readily than creating such sections manually—just remember to update them all before turning in your final deliverable.

One **Pro Tip** that has saved me many an hour of work when a quirkily-formatted table of contents or figures is required is remembering that the table of contents itself is nothing but a list of rules dictating the appearance of the table and what it's indexing. Therefore, if you're required to duplicate the format of a TOC from one document in another document, it's often simple enough to copy the TOC from the first document into the second, perform Update Field so it rebuilds based on the content of the second document, and presto—more often than not, you'll have a properly formatted table with the same appearance as the first but indexing the content of the second.

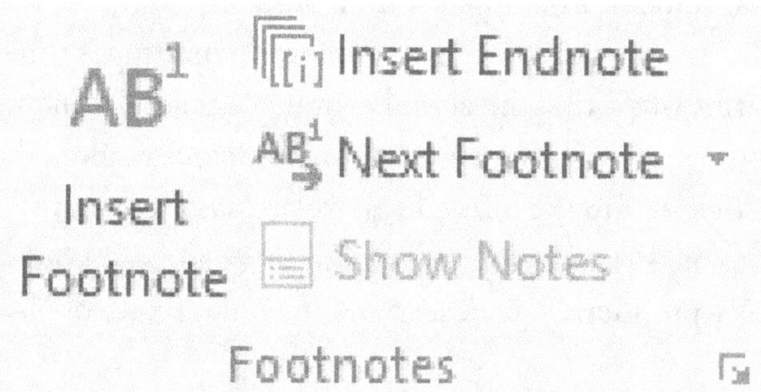

Insert Footnote and **Insert Endnote** function in much the same manner: wherever you have placed the editing cursor within the body of your document at the moment you hit the relevant button, Word will place a reference mark there and jump to either the foot of that page for footnotes or to the end of the document for endnotes[1], where you will be able to enter the text of the appropriate note.

(Should you insert text before your footnote reference and cause it to be moved to another page, Word will automatically move its corresponding note along with it.) Both footnotes and endnotes will appear set off from the primary body text by a separator line, and of course the appearance of the note text can be edited as you choose. Once you have inserted a number of footnotes or endnotes into a document, the **Next Footnote** button and its attached dropdown menu allows you to easily jump from one to the next, via **Next** and **Previous Footnote**, **Next Endnote** and **Previous Endnote**.

For those in legal or other professions whose work requires extensive citation and internal reference, these tools can be a godsend, but I would caution the average user away from unnecessary notation and citations, as such devices can quickly become tiresome, and tend to interrupt the flow of a document's primary content. Just as certain readers of newspapers and magazines inevitably find messages stating a story they started reading on page two is 'continued on page 41' too irritating to bother with and choose to bail out rather than flip back and forth between pages, so too might your reader decide your over-frequent use of foot- or endnotes too precious to merit continuing onward. And consider this: if a particular piece of data isn't important enough to merit mention within the main body of your text, is it worth including at all?

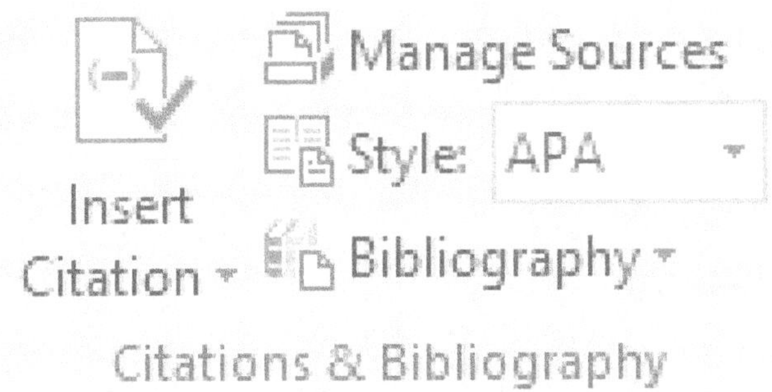

Insert Citation is likely a section you already know whether or not you'll need to use up front; rarely is an average user called upon to create a document featuring citations, while conversely, those whose work requires the use of extensive citations generally gravitate towards use of Word and other word processors specifically to simplify their workflows. If you fall into the latter category, Insert Citation can save hours of painstaking effort; if the former, you can probably skip this section for now.

Put basically, Insert Citation allows you to construct a list of sources, generally formatted in standard APA style by default but with the option of many other citation styles within the **Style** dropdown menu to the right, and featuring fields for all the typical information that should be included in a list of cited sources. Clicking the Insert Citation button brings up a dropdown menu allowing you to add a source; once one or more sources are entered, these sources will appear within the dropdown to allow you to add citations to those sources within the main body of your content with a click.

Once all sources have been entered, **Bibliography** allows you to easily create either a standard Bibliography or list of **Works Cited** in your chosen style by simply placing the cursor within the body of your document where you'd like the bibliography or works cited list to appear and clicking the appropriate button within the dropdown menu.

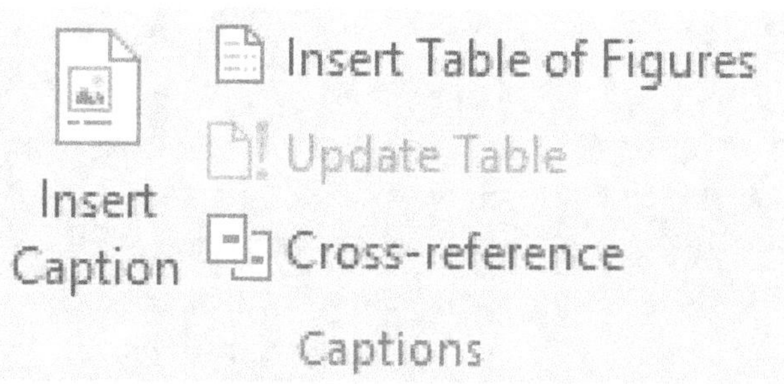

Figure 1: Insert Caption screenshot

The **Captions** section is most useful when the content of your text contains a number of figures or images inserted within the flow of its main body, much like the book you are currently reading. For the sake of simplicity and flow, I have chosen to eschew captions for the most part, but the 'Insert Caption screenshot' caption I've placed above for the sake of illustration should give you an idea how captions generally appear by default. By default, captions are numbered sequentially beginning with Figure 1, but this can be adjusted to various styles such as i, a, I, or A from the **Numbering...** dialog, accessible from within the Insert Caption dialog. As you might expect, **Insert Table of Figures** creates a table of contents-like index to all captioned figures within a document; as noted above, the tool can be accessed from within the Table of Contents dialog, but also appears here as a separate button.

With the introduction of search capabilities within electronic documents and ebooks, the usefulness and prevalence of indexes has been much reduced from the days when print was the sole medium for text. Nevertheless, for those who choose to or must include indexes within their work, Word's **Index** tools dramatically simplify the process, functioning much the same as the other tools described above: **Mark Entry** indicates text that should be indexed, placing a reference mark at that location in much the same manner as a footnote or citation, while **Insert Index** creates the index from all current entries, similar to a table of contents or list of works cited. Because indexes (or indices, depending on your preference—both forms are correct) generally contain page numbers, you must remember to update the index using the **Update Index** button to ensure each reference addresses the proper page once your document is complete, also much like a table of contents.

Finally, Word's **Table of Authorities** section of tools specifically applies to creation of legal briefs and the particular formatting that applies to such legal documents. Although they function in much the same manner as typical citations, the result when using the **Table of Authorities** tools will more closely resemble the typical standard format of such documents without requiring extensive modification. Frankly, unless you work within the legal profession, you should never need to use this section—and if you do, you should probably seek out more specific instruction for your field than a general book such as this. Nevertheless, use of these tools is relatively straightforward, constituting entry of sources cited and marking citations to said sources within the main body of the text, facilitating creation of the very specific document formatting required by courts and other legal authorities.

CHAPTER 12

MAILINGS TAB

THE **MAILINGS** TAB makes me wonder what year users who do use it regularly are living in. Not that mail doesn't exist or isn't important anymore, but if your business involves any kind of mailing on either a large scale or a small one, Word is probably not the ideal tool to meet your needs.

In short, Mailings allows you to use a predefined database to create custom mailings, including envelope and label templates and the type of form-filled mailings that you probably receive regularly, addressed to you but with the distinct tone of being addressed to 'consumer', 'resident', or more likely, 'person from whom we would like to extract money'.

Perhaps the first time this transparent advertising trick was used, it paid significant dividends; today, none but the smallest children get a thrill from seeing their name appear on an impersonal advertising flier. As few will be unaware, widespread concern for privacy and corporate use of personal information is rising, and seen much differently than it was only a few decades ago. When personal data is used cavalierly, it is much more likely to worry your target audience than in years past—and today, unless you have a genuine personal connection with someone, affecting one is more likely to be perceived as unethical or even offensive.

In short, if your business requires use of the tools offered in Mailing, Word's limited and notoriously frustrating abilities are unlikely to serve your needs as well as custom mailing software or advertising tools designed to simplify these chores, most of which can sync with common sales platforms and ticket tracking databases, or simply outsourcing such duties to mass-mailing advertising experts. And if your organization doesn't currently use such tactics, well...perhaps it might be worthwhile to consider strongly whether you should start now.

Quite frankly, even professionals who have been forced to use Word's Mail Merge functions often have trouble navigating its complexities, so I am loath to lead readers down any primrose paths by implying mail merge can be quickly or easily accomplished, even with the aid of a book such as this. Fortunately for those who do wish to make the attempt, Word contains a step-by-step walkthrough of the process on the Mailings tab, beneath Start Mail Merge, appropriately named **Step by Step Mail Merge Wizard**. If you're reading this book, this tool is likely the only one you should be using with regards to the Mailings tab, if any. I understand the temptation may be overwhelming for many, picturing saving themselves hours of time customizing their meticulously crafted holiday letters or party invitations, but I caution you from hard-won experience that you are far more likely to ensnare yourself in a frustrating bind from which you may not be able to extract yourself without many more hours of effort than you might expect.

In short, Mailings is far from a tool for the faint of heart. If you choose to progress further into its intricacies, I highly suggest obtaining expert advice or consultation, whether that be instruction more specifically geared towards its use, or even in-person instruction.

CHAPTER 13
REVIEW TAB

THE **REVIEW** TAB contains a number of tools allowing the user to fine-tune the content of their text via semi-automated **Spelling & Grammar** checks, as well as to collaborate on authorship with one or more other people using **Comments** and **Track Changes** to keep all collaborative parties on the same page for the duration of the document creation process, both figuratively and literally. Speaking honestly, as a professional document creator who is frequently called upon to collaborate with multiple co-authors, the tools contained herein have saved me untold hours of frustration; before the tools available within modern word processors facilitated such collaboration, reconciling multiple drafts submitted by different authors could easily become a job in itself.

Today, remote collaboration via tools such as Google Docs is commonplace and the obstacles posed by long-distance telecommuting become smaller with each year. Yet the essential issues posed by working in such a manner remain significant obstacles for those who haven't learned to navigate Word's powerful review tools—so let's clear up as many of these potentially confusing issues as we can, right now.

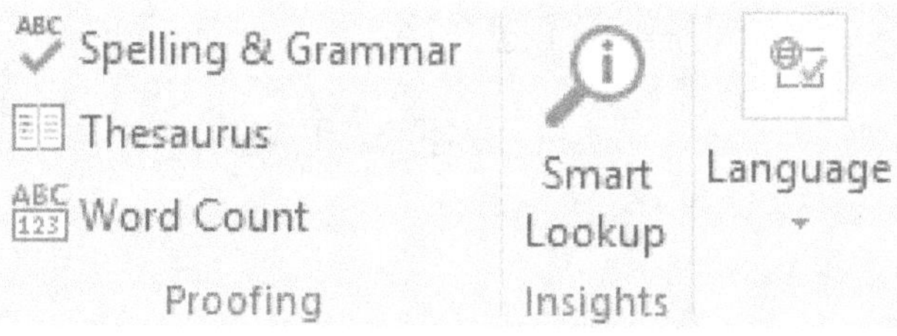

The leftmost section of the Review tab is the only one that doesn't specifically apply to collaboration, and as such it's the one most novice users are most likely to already be familiar with. **Proofing** contains controls for **Spelling & Grammar** checks, both of which should be used frequently by most users. It's a rare document that contains no typographical errors or misused words, and while Word's spelling and grammar checks are far from infallible, their use will nearly always result in a more polished, professional-looking finished product. Take care to pay attention as you perform your spelling and grammar checks, however, as Word is unfortunately still fairly primitive at deriving context and is liable to suggest mistaken substitutions based on its limited ability to understand what you're actually trying to say. Additionally, the program can only identify the limited number of words contained within whichever dictionary you're using as your base of reference, as set by **Language** (see below)—but fortunately, as you use the program and perform more and more spelling checks, you have the opportunity to add words to your installation's custom directory whenever Word stumbles across one it can't identify. This feature comes in highly useful for those of us who work in highly technical fields and whose documents often contain terminology not found in Word's default dictionaries—and unlike most of

Word's features, the more you use it, the more useful it will be to you! You must be doubly certain the word in question is in fact spelled correctly before you add it to your custom dictionary, of course— otherwise, Word will mistakenly pass through your misspelled entry during future spellchecks—so even if you're ninety-five percent certain it's spelled properly, I suggest running a quick search online to confirm your suspicions before clicking **Add to Dictionary**.

Thesaurus is another powerful tool frequently invoked by many users, though I don't believe I've ever actually used the button on the Review tab, instead generally selecting the word in question, right-clicking and choosing **Synonyms** from the pop-up dialog, followed by **Thesaurus** at the bottom of the resulting list, should none of the given synonyms prove acceptable. To be perfectly honest, I would personally prefer Word offered a deeper and more comprehensive choice of words within Thesaurus, but most users are likely to find its selection of words more than adequate to meet their needs.

Pressing the **Word Count** button pops up an informative window displaying a number of useful statistics regarding your document, including numbers of pages, words, characters (both including spaces and not), paragraphs, and lines, with the option to either include or exclude text boxes, footnotes, and endnotes. Depending on your particular settings, the most useful of this information likely appears in your Word window's status bar, at the bottom of the window— particularly number of pages and word count—and as noted previously, you can also find much of this information on the File tab, so unless you are dealing with a document requiring particularly onerous restrictions on page or character count, it's unlikely you'll need this pop-up often.

Smart Lookup in the Review tab's Insights section is Microsoft's attempt to steer as much traffic to their Bing search engine as possible from within their own products, and is largely intended to supplant the typical "Google search for an answer" procedure most are probably already used to using. I suppose some might find the ability to search from within Word rather than opening a browser convenient, particularly if Bing is their search engine of choice, but I suspect the overwhelming majority of users would be better served by sticking with whatever procedure they generally use to locate information online, as I haven't found the feature either particularly smart or insightful.

Language allows the user to select the set of rules by which the Spelling & Grammar checks operate; as a reader of this book, I suspect 'English (U.S.)' will be set as the default, but depending on the audience of your document you may need to choose any of the many options Word offers, from Afrikaans to Yoruba. Fortunately, Word's 'Detect language automatically' option is generally checked by default, so even if you find yourself working in an unfamiliar context Word should adjust itself without assistance, but if you find your spelling and grammar checks flagging an unusual number of instances you know to be correct, it may be worth checking to see whether Language is properly set for your present document.

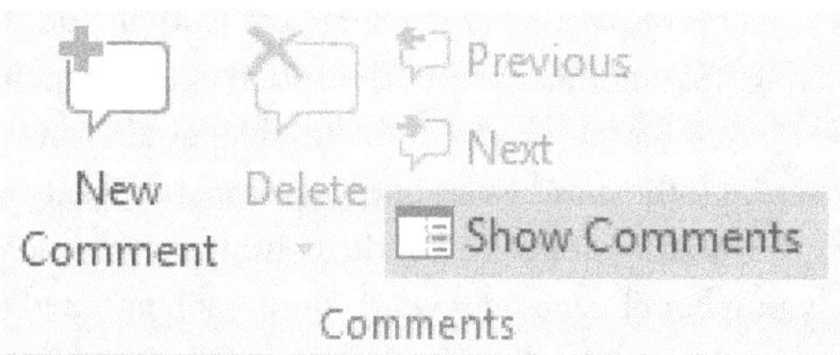

Comments are the least intrusive of Word's collaborative tools, in that they allow users to select sections of text and insert their related thoughts without actually modifying the content of the document itself. This can be particularly useful when one collaborator isn't completely certain what another is trying to say within a particular section, and thus doesn't feel comfortable progressing further without clarification. Once **Show Comments** is selected, all comments within a document will appear off the right of the text, making it appear as if the document's margins are wider than necessary. Don't worry—inserting comments doesn't actually change the dimensions of your document, and unless specifically directed otherwise comments will not be visible in the finalized document or when printed. Using **Previous** and **Next**, Word makes it easy to jump from one comment to the next, addressing your collaborator's commented concerns and then clicking **Delete** to remove each comment as its concerns are addressed. While I can't tell you collaboration is always easy, I can say that Word comments are some of the most helpful tools in minimizing unnecessary conflict—at least, when all parties involved can eventually come to an agreement on how each commented issue should be resolved! For these reasons, Word comments are generally most useful when one person can be identified as the primary author of a document, while others may simply contribute their thoughts along the development process. But at the very least, comments allow them a voice—and sometimes, that's enough.

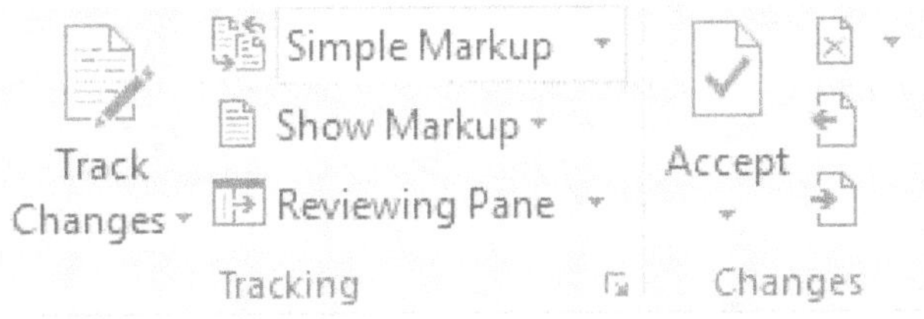

For documents that involve a deeper degree of co-authoring, the **Tracking** tools will probably be of more use. Change tracking can be a fairly involved process, though in principle it's actually quite straightforward: by clicking the **Track Changes** dropdown, a user can select **Track Changes** to turn change tracking on for that document. From that point forward, any alterations to that document will register as a tracked change, noted with the user name of the person who made the change in question as set under Word's

General options. That document can then be sent to other collaborators whose changes will also be tracked and noted with their respective usernames, or returned to the first user, who will then have the opportunity to review each tracked change made to the document and decide whether or not to accept or reject each change in turn using the tools within the **Changes** section.

Using both tracked changes and comments, any number of co-authoring concerns can be addressed in a highly efficient manner, eliminating the need for co-authors to sit down side-by-side in real time, either virtually or literally. Again, I would suggest maintaining a series of numbered and dated backups in case you find your collaborators accepting or deleting changes you might disagree with, but once you grow comfortable with the change tracking process, you'll wonder how you ever got by without it.

Of course, as you likely know, whenever collaboration between humans occurs it's possible for things to go awry. Even with the powerful tools offered by comments and change tracking, the process of collaboration can still get tangled up and create seemingly insurmountable confusions—say, for example, a collaborator forgets to turn Track Changes on, either mistakenly or intentionally, or two collaborators working simultaneously on different copies of the same document come up with conflicting versions of the same section. In these instances, **Compare** can be a lifesaver by offering the option to either **Compare** two versions of the same document and highlighting the differences between them or to **Combine** revisions from multiple authors into a single document. Frankly, these processes can sometimes be difficult even for experienced Word users and should therefore be left as a last resort when you find yourself with a Gordian knot of a document you cannot untangle any other way, but it's nice to know the tools are there to back you up if necessary. I can attest that they've saved me from a sleepless night or two!

If you have the authority to apply them, the options under **Protect** might help you avoid such gridlocks, offering the ability to restrict other users from either changing the content of the document or limiting them to a specified set of changes such as inserting comments or tracked changes, or even disallowing any actions but filling in forms. Slightly less useful is the ability to limit users to a restricted list of styles, but otherwise enforcing the options offered by document protection might help keep your project from running off the rails, particularly if you're working with an individual who has proven unable to stay within certain boundaries in the past. In most cases I'd advise against preemptively applying protection to Word documents unless you have specific reasons for doing so, as the Word document restrictions are infrequently used enough to confuse users who haven't encountered them before and maintaining proper backups and document development control are generally sufficient in most cases—but it's inarguable that there are situations where the use of such protection may well prove necessary. (I can think of two or three from my own experience without even trying, but I'll spare you the gruesome details.)

Finally, the **Linked Notes OneNote** section offers the ability to integrate with Microsoft's OneNote service—and like Smart Lookup, essentially forces use of Microsoft's service on the user rather than offering any options that might be more conducive to their individual workflow, such as integration with Evernote or other note-taking services. If you are already a user of OneNote and comfortable with using the service as part of your daily workflow, you might find Linked Notes useful to you. As I am not a OneNote user and don't plan to become one anytime soon, I can't recommend the average user commit to Microsoft's transparent attempt to favor its own products above end-user functionality.

CHAPTER 14

VIEW TAB

THE **VIEW** TAB is placed somewhat unintuitively, in my opinion. At far right, it can easily be overlooked or considered the least important by position alone, and by its placement beside the **Review** tab the visual similarity between the words can imply an interfunctionality that the tabs don't bear out.

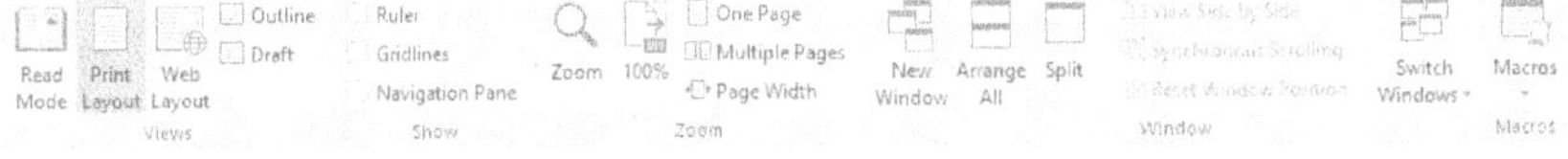

Frankly, the **View** tab may be the single most important tab in terms of controlling your own personal experience of using the program and knowing how your document will appear to your end reader. For this reason, I'd argue it might better be placed much further left, perhaps even between the Home and Insert tabs—though the logic of its current placement seems based on document appearance as an element of document finalization, in practical use the View tab is most useful during active document editing.

In most cases you'll be interacting with your document in the **Print Layout** view—the view in which each page of your document appears separately, divided by a gray background as shown below, but the section at furthest left allows the user to toggle between a selection of different **Views**.

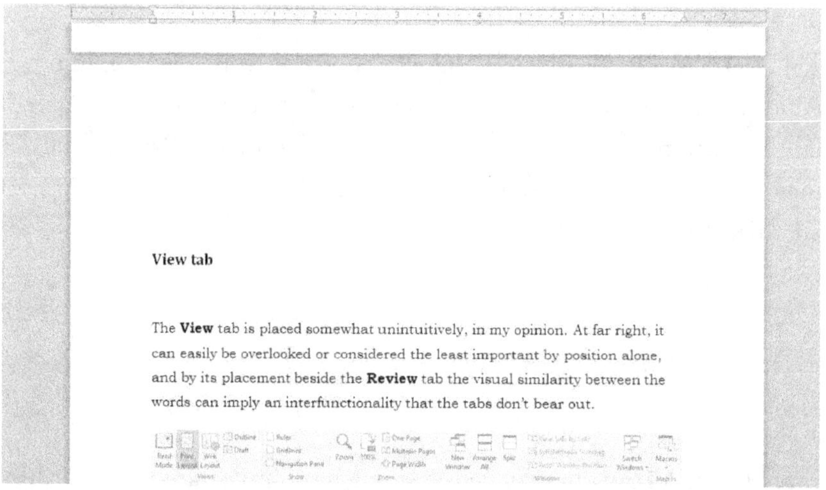

Read Mode is most useful when a .doc or .docx is being treated as a finished ebook, rather than using the more common .epub and .mobi ebook formats, or PDF. While this practice is not as common as in times past, before the proliferation of ebooks and standardization of consumer ebook formats, **Read Mode** can still be useful to streamline your reading experience or provide a change of perspective when proofreading your document, your eyes already weary from endlessly poring over its **Print Layout** view.

Web Layout may be useful to you if you are writing specifically for online use or if you're interested in editing your document as a continuous scroll, rather than as its separate pages—though this latter goal can be accomplished via the **Draft** view as well. In practical effect, most users will see little difference between the **Web Layout** and **Draft** views, as the two look and function so identically one wonders why they weren't combined into a single view with an option to toggle between the minor display options specific to either view. Nevertheless, as noted above, a change of perspective is always useful in the line-by-line proofreading portion of the writing process —a part that is just as important as ever, in spite of the array of tools Word offers to streamline and simplify it—and certain documents with complex formatting can only be efficiently handled from within the Draft view. However, the overwhelming majority of users will never encounter a Word document of such complexity, and should feel content to ignore the **Web Layout** and **Draft** views with impunity—in nearly all situations, the **Print Layout** view provides both the clearest idea how your document will appear and the most intuitive, comprehensible editing interface.

Outline view, conversely, is a subject in and of itself; uniquely to the **Views** options, **Outline** activates its own 'hidden' tab, effectively overlaying **Outline** view on top of the current document view and engaging an entirely separate set of editing tools specifically for outlines. Unique to the View tab, this 'hidden' tab behavior leads us to cover the **Outlining** tab in a separate section for such 'hidden' tabs and menus.

> ☐ Ruler
>
> ☐ Gridlines
>
> ☐ Navigation Pane
>
> Show

To the right of the **Views** section, **Show** features options for toggling three quite different elements of Word's visual interface. **Ruler** allows the user to toggle the appearance of the ruler atop the Word page editing window on and off—I always keep it on in order to most effectively manage tabs, margins, and other such page elements, and it is hardly very intrusive to keep it on, but if you prefer the cleaner look of the interface without the ruler, unchecking the box here will get rid of it. The **Gridlines** are rarely helpful except when engaging in intensive layout or design, but can be useful when aligning visual elements manually. Leaving them on longer than it takes to solve whatever graphic design problem one is attempting to solve would seem fairly intolerable, though, as intrusive as the gridlines are, and most users will likely never need them. Finally, when the **Navigation Pane** is turned on it appears as a sidebar at the left side of the Word window, auto-populating with links to sections of the document as defined by its headings and offering options to browse pages by thumbnail images, search within the document, or jump forward or backward to the next heading using the arrow buttons. Note that user-defined bookmarks will **not** appear within the **Navigation Pane**—a primary reason I consider bookmarks as implemented within Word to be near-useless.

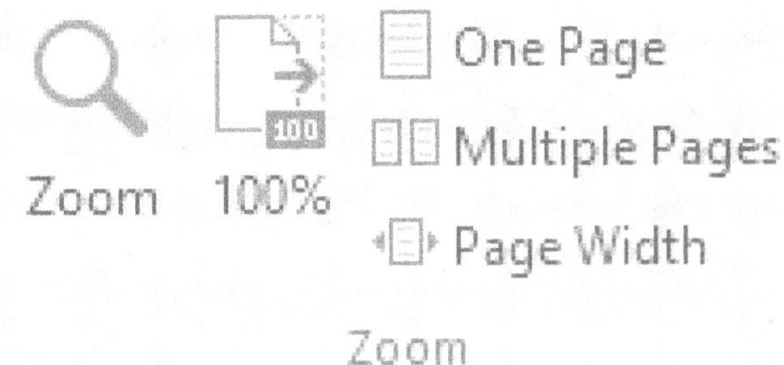

Zoom contains a number of controls for tailoring the apparent size of your document within the Word window, including presets for **200%** actual size, **100%**, **75%**, **Page Width**, **Text Width**, or to fit the entire page within the window, either by itself in the **One Page** view or side-by-side with its neighbor in the **Two Pages** view. You can also select the exact percentage of zoom within the Zoom dialog box, though it's important to remember none of these choices change the appearance of the document itself, only your interface to work with it. Therefore, the only correct view to choose is the view that you're most comfortable with. If the size and resolution of your monitor permits and you prefer to see an entire page at once, the full- or two-page view might fit your needs; however, if you're limited to the size of a typical laptop screen, the dimensions of a typical page are likely to render its contents illegible in either full-page view. Alternately, those of us whose eyesight is less than perfect might elect to work **Page Width** view, **Text Width** view, **200%** actual size or even greater, depending on the size of the document and the fonts therein.

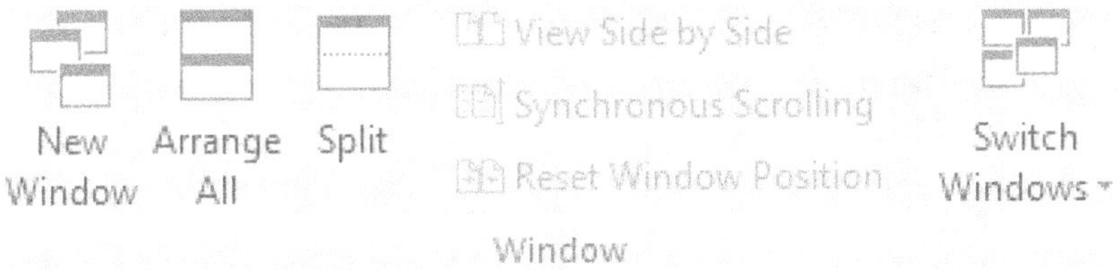

The **Window** section allows you to create multiple viewpoints to the same document, allowing you to view and edit separate sections of the document side by side in separate **New Windows** or splitting the current window into top and bottom sections, each providing a view to a different part of the document. To place a **Split**, click the **Split** button and then click within the document to place the split where you'd like—the top and bottom split section can be as large or as small as the dimensions of your monitor and your document allow. A split can also be placed by clicking the small minus icon atop the right-hand scroll bar, just below the ribbon, and dragging it down to your chosen dividing spot.

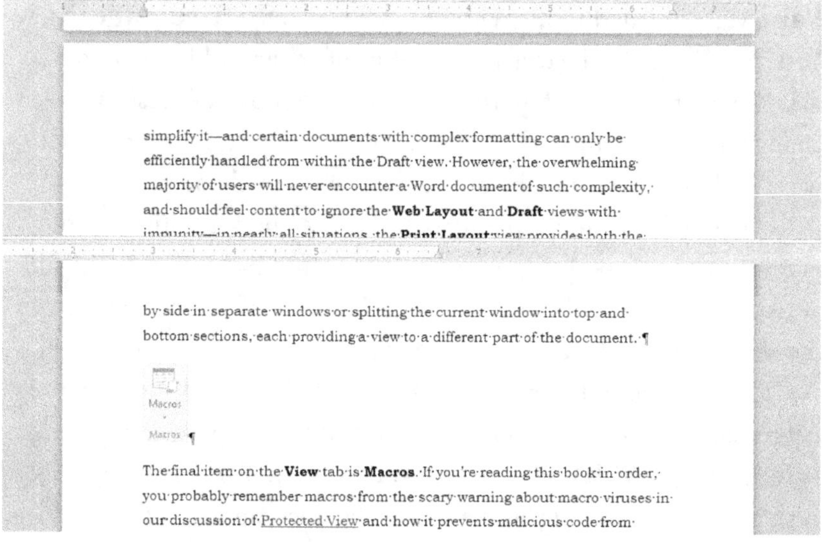

Once a **Split** is placed in the current window, the Split button changes to **Remove Split** to remove the bottom split section and return to the standard view; alternately, you can click on the divider marking the split and drag it to the top or bottom of the window to enlarge either split section to become the standard view. To remove a **New Window**, simply click its top corner 'x' to close it as you would any standard window.

Both the split screen and New Window tools can prove extremely useful, particularly when working with long documents in which sections often refer to each other: rather than constantly scrolling up or down to check one item or another or ensure consistency, you can place all relevant sections on your screen for easy reference at all times. Of course, you will find usability governed by your available monitor space—as a professional technical writer with a dual-monitor setup, I can place two windows side-by-side quite easily and even maintain three or four different windows to the same document without straining the limits of my desktop, but when I'm working with my Macbook Air laptop these techniques are somewhat less helpful on its comparatively tiny thirteen-inch screen. In these situations, Split allows the maximum amount of information density while maintaining comprehensibility—even if you're limited to two views, you'll quickly find managing multiple windows gets confusing rapidly when you're working with such a restricted workspace.

The final item on the **View** tab is **Macros**. If you're reading this book in order, you probably remember macros from the scary warning about macro viruses in our discussion of Protected View and how it prevents malicious code from automatically running when a document is opened. Essentially, a macro is a piece of Virtual Basic programming code that acts on the content of your Word document. When implemented by experts and used properly, macros can save many hours of work by bundling several frequently performed steps into one—but because macros are so powerful, they can cause complications and problems as well.

Frankly, even elementary use of **Macros** constitutes an advanced use of Microsoft Word 2016 that lies well outside the scope of this book and beyond the needs of all but the most demanding user—even the massive, everything-you'd-ever-want-to-know-about-Microsoft Word instructional tomes rarely cover macros in much detail due to the potential for confusion. Basically, a macro 'records' a series of actions performed by the user and renders those actions as a repeatable piece of code that can be applied at will, either through the Macros dialog or by assigning it to a unique keystroke combination. Any Word document that contains a macro must be saved with the unique file extension .docm, alerting the user (and Word) that the document should be handled with care.

The fact that Microsoft felt it necessary to escalate careful handling of macro-embedded files to the level of splitting them off into their own file extension should give you some idea of the potential security risk macros can represent. In most cases, you won't want to either send or receive .docm files; unless it has been pre-established that you will be working with macros, there is good reason to be leery of macros you haven't created yourself, and chances are very low you're creating your own macros if you're reading this book. If you do find macros helpful in your workflow, I suggest using them to author your document and then saving to the normal .docx format to remove the macros before delivering it to the end user. In the rare case you will be collaborating on a macro-enabled document with another user, be sure to alert them to the validity of your .docm file before sending it to them. Otherwise, you might find yourself on the receiving end of some (perfectly valid) questions about your personal security practices!

CHAPTER 15

TELL ME...

THE **TELL ME...** box appears in line with the tabs atop the
ribbon, but it is not a tab itself. Rather, if you click on the box you can
type questions in natural language to find answers to your questions
about using Word—for example, 'Tell me about inserting pictures
into my document' or 'Tell me how to choose number of columns.'

One assumes the feature's name and prompt were chosen to guide
the novice user to the use of natural language sentence construction,
though I wonder if the loss of clarity conveyed by the simple, univer-
sally-understood word 'Help' is worth the tradeoff. Given an average

user with low levels of familiarity using a program, I would guess more would instantly know what a section designated 'Help' is for, while 'Tell me...' seems comparatively clumsy and far less direct.

Nevertheless, **Tell Me...** does offer one benefit other methods of finding assistance—including this book—cannot: search results can bring up actions and commands that can be directly applied to your document from within the results dialog box. For instance, the 'Tell me about inserting pictures into my document' is likely to bring up the 'Insert Object' option, through which you can solve your problem without having to click back over to the Insert tab.

This advantage makes **Tell Me...** significantly more useful for the novice user who may not remember on which tab every command is located, even after reading this book—if one's memory and a few seconds of cursory clicking fails to locate the specific command you need at that moment, **Tell Me...** might allow you to find it, apply the solution, and get back to work relatively quickly. The problem with this, of course, is that while the immediate problem has been solved, that solution wasn't necessarily communicated fully to the user—so the next time that particular issue arises, that user may find him- or herself relying on **Tell Me...** again and again, in essence using the search box as an inefficient crutch to avoid having to learn anything new and maintaining a suboptimal workflow.

If you find yourself falling into this trap, I suggest taking the moment or two necessary to learn the proper procedures suggested by your search results rather than blindly relying on **Tell Me...** to lead you where you need to go. For rarely-used commands and occasional formatting necessities, **Tell Me...** can be a huge timesaver, particularly for the user who is rarely called to step outside of their comfort zone—but don't let what may initially seem like the easiest route become an obstacle to expanding your skills.

CHAPTER 16

SHARE TAB

THE **SHARE** TAB is a proprietary method of collaboration that relies on integration with OneDrive, Microsoft's DropBox-like cloud storage file hosting service, or SharePoint, their corporate collaboration service. Most users reading this book will probably have OneDrive accounts already due to the aggressive tactics used by Windows 10's upgrade and installation process, but if not it's easy enough—and free—to sign up for one at http://onedrive.live.com. Free accounts come with a limited amount of space (5GB as of this writing) but this is more than sufficient for Word .docx files, which are typically sized in exponentially smaller kilobytes (KB) or megabytes (MB). In decades of professional technical writing I have never encountered a Word document so sizeable as to register in the gigabyte scale, but I can't imagine that document would be particularly stable or workable so I'm far from anxious to make the attempt.

In any case, once a shared folder has been designated within your OneDrive folder, files can be saved to that cloud folder and shared from within Word's Share tools to any number of collaborators, each of whom will then be granted access to edit the document. (Note that these edits will only affect the copy of your document placed into your OneDrive shared folder, not any other copy of the file stored elsewhere on your local machine.)

As the users you've granted access to the document edit it, you'll be able to see changes in real time from within the Share tool to facilitate long-distance collaboration—for instance, two or more users can share a single document while chatting on the phone, each adding their changes and edits as they go, resulting in a single final document containing everyone's input. Without Share or a similar collaboration tool, the process of reconciling and combining edits and changes produced by multiple authors can easily become a job in itself.

The problem with **Share** is a typical one for Microsoft products: it's only designed to integrate readily with other Microsoft products. As implemented within Word, you will likely find the most success using Share within small groups in which you can be absolutely certain each user has a legitimate and current version of Microsoft Word 2016 as well as an active Microsoft login and OneDrive account. Unfortunately, most organizations with an ongoing need for elec-tronic collaboration are likely to invest in one specific platform to simplify their internal processes—which may or may not be compatible with Word 2016. If you're accustomed to collaborating via Google Docs or Dropbox—services I've encountered far more often than Microsoft's comparable products in the course of my duties—you'll find Word offers little to help you. Should you choose to attempt to use Share for collaboration, be prepared to explain to each of your collaborators why they must have a Microsoft account to do so and why using Word sharing will be superior to their customary methods of working.

While it's difficult to blame Microsoft for attempting to leverage Word and Office's incredible market penetration to bolster their less-successful endeavors, unfortunately their execution of these features within Word 2016 limits the program's usability so severely as to make it effectively useless in most professional capacities. Granted, their argument that maintaining interoperability with a number of different non-Microsoft filesharing services might prove prohibitively difficult does hold some validity, yet in a world in which numerous apps on the average user's phone successfully maintain a comparable level of compatibility the subtle differences are difficult to discern. Suffice to say, Microsoft chooses not to open in-Word collaboration to a wider range of services, which is entirely their choice—but until they do, it's unlikely Word's Share feature will garner more than a tiny slice of the collaboration pie.

CHAPTER 17

SPECIAL CASE-SPECIFIC TABS: OUTLINING, BLOG POST, PICTURE/DRAWING TOOLS, AND DEVELOPER

WAIT—HAVEN'T we already covered all the tabs that typically appear atop the ribbon? Indeed we have—but certain tricky tabs only appear when activated by specific conditions. Confusing? Some might say so! I can't say for certain why Microsoft chose to have these 'special' tabs function in such a nonintuitive manner, but now that you're aware of their idiosyncrasies you will be prepared to deal with them if necessary.

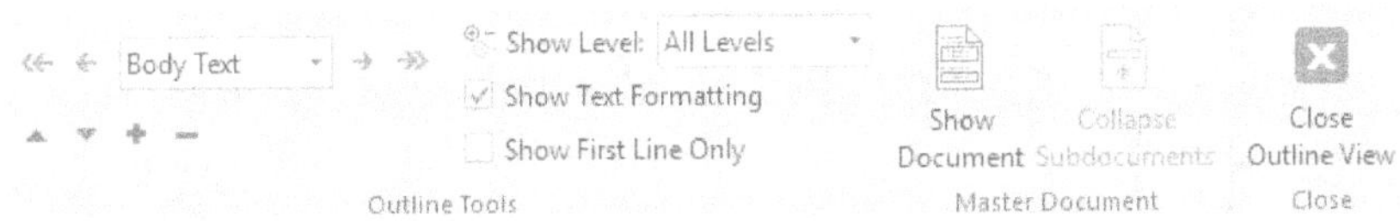

The **Outlining** tab shows up when **Outline** view is engaged on the **View** tab, appearing between the **File** and **Home** tabs while **Outline** view is active, as discussed earlier.

Blog Post appears in place of the home tab when 'Blog Post' is selected as the document type when creating a new document and is intended to function as a seamless interface between Word and your blogging platform of choice. However, while this feature was only introduced to Word relatively recently, anecdotal evidence suggests Microsoft may no longer be committed to maintaining it; many users have encountered issues attempting to use Word with blogging platforms not owned or controlled by Microsoft, a situation that seems unlikely to change, particularly as the popularity of blogging as a whole has declined significantly since the days when changing tides seemed to demand the feature's addition. (If you search online for information on using the Blog Post tools, you will find most originates from when the features were first introduced and few have so much as bothered to take notice in the intervening years.)

Frankly, I would not be at all surprised to see the Blog Post toolbar and its related tools vanish in an upcoming version of Word, or at least deemphasized and buried behind additional menus or tabs. Even if you do use a Microsoft-based blogging platform and hope to replace your platform's built-in editing features with Word's Blog Post tools, I suspect you may find its deficiencies in integration with blog management and other administrative duties may offset any perceived gains, but if you frequently blog with advanced formatting you find difficult to execute using traditional blog platforms, Word might be worth experimenting with.

When an image that has been inserted into the document has been highlighted, depending on its format either the **Picture Tools Format** tab or the **Drawing Tools Format** tab appears above the ribbon, allowing you to tweak and edit the image as well as arrange it within the text and choose how it interacts with the text around it. In most situations, you will find much greater success editing images outside of Word with dedicated image editing software before inserting the finished image into a Word document; additionally, it is often advantageous to be able to supply edited images separate from the document in which they're contained, such as when required for submission by an editor or publisher. For these and other reasons, I would suggest Word's image editing tools be restricted to limited use, for minor tweaks and adjustments to fit with the flow of a document only. Similarly, in the majority of cases the default **In Line with Text** option will be most appropriate, and though you can also elect for text to run in front of or behind images, it's generally best to err on the side of greater clarity, not only for your reader's sake but for your own.

The **Developer** tab only appears when specifically turned on via an option tucked away under the Customize Ribbon option on the Word Options dialog box, and as its name indicates, it is intended for users creating plugins, add-ons, macros and other customized, highly specified items for and with Word. Frankly, if you're reading this book, you don't need and shouldn't touch the **Developer** tab, and if you do have a legitimate use for the tools therein, you don't need this book.

CHAPTER 18

PUTTING IT ALL TOGETHER

AS YOU'VE UNDOUBTEDLY NOTICED over the course of this book so far, no single tab of the ribbon is likely to contain every function you'll need even for the creation of the simplest of documents. And obviously, you don't want to pull this book out every time you need to remember how to perform actions you use every time you work with Word, so I highly suggest committing to memory the locations of your most frequently used commands.

Fortunately, the repetitive use of a familiar command will cause it to embed itself in your brain even more readily than formal study—so really, all you have to do to become as expert a Microsoft Word 2016 user as you'd like is to use the program and keep using it! Of course, if all you do is repeat the same ten or fifteen functions, you won't really be learning anything new about the program—but then, if you're getting your work done as quickly and efficiently as possible, is it important that you learn more about Word itself?

The authors of some instructional books on Microsoft Word 2016 would have you believe you aren't really using the program to its fullest extent until you have embedded your own macros, configured custom-tailored menus, and defined styles for every conceivable occasion. This is, perhaps, understandable, given the source—but I would suggest that unless you intend to write a book or teach a class on Microsoft Word itself, if you know enough to get your work done, that's good enough for the vast majority of people.

Don't get me wrong; I'm not saying there isn't a need for these Word obsessives or their massive, encyclopedic books. In fact, I would suggest that it might be worth your time and money to invest in one of those thick, all-encompassing volumes to place alongside this one, for those occasions when you do need to research the obscurities of Word for one reason or another. But unless you find the program itself is impeding your progress in some specific way, be careful: as most writers know, getting distracted by minor research points is a surefire recipe for procrastination, justified on a flimsy pretext of education.

So let's quickly review the tabs and the basic tools you'll be most likely to use from each:

- The **File** tab features options for saving, printing, and exporting documents, as well as access to Word's advanced option menus.
- The **Home** tab contains most of the controls and tools you'll use while actively editing the text of your document and its appearance.
- The **Insert** tab offers tools for controlling the non-text elements of your document, such as images and tables, as well as intra-document references and features such as headers, footers, and page numbering.
- The **Design** tab lets you control the document's overall appearance via Themes if you should so choose, but can otherwise be ignored unless you need to insert a background watermark.
- The **Layout** tab allows fine-tuning of a document's

margins and control of how text interacts with non-text elements such as images.

- The **References** tab lets you insert tables of contents, footnotes, endnotes, indexes, and other self-referential features, along with lists of citations and authorities for those whose work requires such.
- The **Mailings** tab should probably be left alone, but can be integrated with databases to create customized mailings, labels and the like.
- The **Review** tab contains the spelling and grammar check controls, along with a number of tools to facilitate collaboration among multiple parties, including comments, tracked changes, and the ability to restrict alterations to a document.
- The **View** tab lets you change your visual interface to fit your workflow, whether that means seeing the document as it would appear when printed, splitting your screen into two views into different sections of the same document, or even creating multiple windows.
- **Tell Me…** is a glorified Help interface.
- **Share** is Microsoft's proprietary OneDrive-based online collaboration interface.

That isn't quite as intimidating as it might initially have seemed, is it? And sure, the list above may not be completely exhaustive, but after reading to this point you probably have a pretty good idea where to find many of the less common commands or tools you might need, or at least where to start looking. And if that fails, you should know by now that **Tell Me…** can help point you in the right direction, so a certain amount of that anxiety in the pit of your stomach should have dissipated. No, you may not have an encyclopedic command of every obscure feature Microsoft Word 2016 may offer—but I can confide with all assurance that very, very few people will ever need to.

Using the basic commands above along with a handful of additional tools will be enough for all but the most demanding Word user's needs, allowing him or her to construct an efficient workflow that serves their needs without allowing Word's complexity to slow their productivity. What seemed confusing and unnatural at first soon becomes second nature, and eventually you'll wonder how you ever did without it!

AFTERWORD

Now that we've reached the end of the ***Get to the Point!* Guide to Microsoft Word 2016**, you should have a functional, working command of most of the general functions you'll need to use in Microsoft Word on a daily basis, if not ninety-nine percent of the time you sit down in front of the computer.

For that one in a hundred occasion when things go wrong and the answer lies outside the scope of this slim book, I encourage you to find the answer yourself by searching online, sticking to reliable sources and using your best judgment at all times—for while no book can prepare you for all of the thousand or more things that can go askew with Microsoft Word or other Office products, no feeling compares with that of digging yourself out of a seemingly desperate hole—and having the confidence to know with certainty that you could do so again, should the occasion recur.

I hope you've found our time together not only informative but entertaining; in today's increasingly frenetic world, time is truly the most valuable commodity we have. If I have one goal for this book, it's that it saves people time—and now that you should be able to get on with your work without wasting half your day struggling with the computer, I hope you use the time you save to reach your personal goals more quickly and efficiently than otherwise. Once this is the case, I'll feel my work has truly been accomplished.

Finally, let me leave you with this one last thought: Microsoft Word is such a massive, powerful program, I sometimes wonder if even the engineers who are no doubt already working on the next iteration of the program have a comprehensive knowledge of its features. As mentioned earlier in this book, I have never run across any book that can truly claim to be fully comprehensive as far as covering every aspect of the program—even the thick, telephone-book sized tomes generally shy away from attempting even a cursory explanation of macros, for example. So don't be afraid to spend some time playing around with the program and testing out various options, including those I've suggested few will have any use for within the text of this book—because who knows? You might just find the one tool that makes your workday easier—and in the end, that's what it's all about.

NOTES

11. REFERENCES TAB

1. Like so.

www.ingramcontent.com/pod-product-compliance
Lightning Source LLC
Chambersburg PA
CBHW071212130726
47998CB00002B/721